RFK—Marked For Death

'Another Son Sacrificed'

Gary Fannin & Tim Brennan

RFK—Marked For Death may be purchased in bulk at special discounts for educational purposes. For conferences or guest speaking on this book or topic, please contact the authors at: jfkbooks1963@yahoo.com.

Visit our website at www.thejfkassassination.com.

Library of Congress Cataloging-in-Publication Data is available on file.
ISBN: 979-8-9883705-0-5

Printed by Cornerstone Publishing in Kennesaw, GA.

RFK—Marked For Death

'Another Son Sacrificed'

This book is lovingly dedicated to my biggest supporter.

My wife, Ann Marie.

And our children Zachary & Caroline.

May the truth, printed within this book,
come out in their lifetime by the U.S. Government

Gary Fannin—June 2023

My life-long quest for the truth has yielded friendships with many first-generation researchers whom I genuinely admire. As of this writing, I believe there are only three alive:

Robert Groden

J. Gary Shaw

Josiah 'Tink' Thompson

Thank you for accepting my friendship, research and supporting my work. I will forever be indebted to all of you.

I would like to thank the following friends/researchers who have supported my endeavors in the past and hopefully the future.

Barr McClellan, Mark Lane, Douglas Caddy, Dr. Cyril Wecht, Ed Tatro, Vince Palamara, Jim Jenkins, Saint John Hunt Mary Ann Moorman Krahmer, Charles & Beverly Oliver Massegee, Marshal Evans, Hubert Clark, Phil Singer, John Barbour, Phillip Nelson, Dick Russell, Oliver Stone, Abraham Bolden, Randy Benson, Judyth Vary Baker, Bud Fensterwald, James Douglass, Harold Weisberg, Penn Jones Jr., Larry Howard, Larry Harris, Andrew Kreig, Janet Hurley Groden, John Judge, L. Fletcher Prouty, Mary Ferrell, Brian Edwards, Casey Quinlan, David Knight, Jefferson Morley, Douglas Horne, Brent Holland Gaeton & Marie Fonzi, Chris & Sharon Gallop, Roger Stone, Steve Cameron, David Denton, Damon Ise, Brian Lloyd, Jim Gochenaur, Barbara Honegger, Scott Reid, Jim Maze Heather Tarver-Fear, Ruthann Starkey-Shipley, Robert Morrow Dr. Michael & Kelly Marcades, William Matson Law, Jim DiEugenio, Kris Millegan and my dear friend, Tim Brennan.

Gary Fannin, June 2023

This book is dedicated to the thousands of individuals and families who have needlessly suffered at the hands of vicious organizations and individuals willing to take the lives of anyone who they believe may be a threat or an obstacle to the self-serving goals they hope to achieve. It is terrifying to think that many of these people hold positions in the highest echelons of American government, because in many cases they have the ability to operate with impunity, erase all footprints of anything that might be traced back to them, saunter about in total arrogance and plan their next crimes. This has happened and will continue to happen in our beloved United States of America, until our citizens rise up collectively, regardless of political affiliation and demand justice.

I cannot say with certainty that there is a God. What I can say is the God I was taught to believe in is overdue to deliver a reckoning to this evil among us.

Tim Brennan—June 2023

Praise for RFK—Marked For Death

Gary Fannin and Tim Brennan have been investigating the assassination of President Kennedy for many years. I am happy to see that they have now published this book about Senator Robert F. Kennedy's assassination as well. The RFK assassination is clearly as much of an unsolved mystery as the murder of his brother John. Not enough has been researched about the assassination. Gary and Tim's work is a fresh look at the murder.

The Robert Kennedy assassination is something that people should care deeply about, especially younger people who are quite deeply affected by the murder of the man who would most probably have been the next President of the United States and would have ended the Vietnam war years earlier, saving countless lives. The world needs to think and learn more about the RFK case and understand what questions that still need to be answered about the 1968 murder of a truly great man.

Robert J. Groden, author/researcher who released The Zapruder Film on Geraldo Rivera's 'Late Night America,' March 6, 1975.

For over 40 years, I have joined others in excavating truth; particularly related to surreptitious, yet emboldened truth related to the assassinations of courageous politicians like President John F. Kennedy (d. 1963), his brother, Senator and United States Attorney General Robert Francis Kennedy (d. 1968), American preacher and civil rights revolutionary activist Martin Luther King, Jr. (d. 1968) and other far less valued individuals, whose deaths were easily swept under the carpet of passing time.

Never have I been more impressed by deeply researched, documented truths as revealed in **RFK - *Marked for Death*** by researchers/authors Gary Fannin and Tim Brennan. Those who have little time for fluff will find themselves mesmerized by their narrative covering Kennedy assassinations and even reaching into 9/11 illogical and mysterious "facts" heralded by our government.

Seasoned American adults and young, perhaps less-informed truth seekers alike, are encouraged to explore Fannin and Brennan's outstanding work.

Michael Marcades, PhD, Son of Rose Cherami, author,
ROSE CHERAMI: Gathering Fallen Petals, Revised Second Edition.

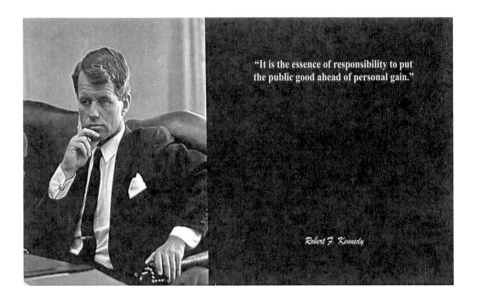

"It is the essence of responsibility to put the public good ahead of personal gain."

Robert F. Kennedy

One

Foreword

"Power tends to corrupt; absolute power corrupts absolutely"—Lord Acton, British historian. In America, the best example of this truism is the CIA. On September 18, 1947 the CIA was founded by President Harry S. Truman. The original purpose of the CIA was to coordinate Government intelligence efforts. The Hydra that the CIA became and still is today was never envisioned or imagined. Almost from its inception they became answerable to no one, funded their black-ops operations globally, toppled governments worldwide through assassinations of world leaders and over time gained complete control of American media through Operation Mockingbird. Several years after he left the Presidency, Truman remarked, "I never would have agreed to the formulation of the Central Intelligence Agency back in forty-seven, if I had known it would become the American Gestapo."

Taken on its own, the fact that an ex-CIA Director, George H. W. Bush became President is scary enough, but when Ronald Reagan became President in 1981 and assembled his Cabinet for the first time, he asked William Casey, then Director of the CIA, what his goals for the CIA were. As preposterous and incredulous as it might seem he responded, "We'll know our disinformation program is complete when everything the American public believes is false." The very purpose of Operation Mockingbird was—and still is—to have CIA operatives within the staffs of every major American media outlet, to control everything the American public sees and hears. It doesn't matter if your political affiliation leans towards CNN or FOX, the CIA is telling them both what to say.

Horrifyingly, control of the media did not satisfy the CIA's unquenchable thirst for power and control, and they decided to control U.S. Government at the highest levels. Anyone and everyone who favored an agenda that might impair their objectives would be – and was – eliminated. Look no further than the assassinations of John F. Kennedy, Robert F. Kennedy, Dr. Martin Luther King, Malcolm X and numerous others for proof. Their involvement in these heinous atrocities against our own Government is irrefutable.

Robert F. Kennedy stood no chance whatsoever of becoming President. Much like JFK was led into a killing zone at Dealey Plaza, RFK was led into a killing zone at the Ambassador Hotel kitchen. The planners also made sure no professional photographers would be in either location. There were numerous organizations and individuals who made certain of that. What were RFK's grievous sins that would cause these forces to come together as they had five years earlier to murder his Brother? Like JFK, he wanted to remove America from the Vietnam War, which would have cost The American Industrial Military complex and Texas Big Oil millions of dollars. He wanted to continue his assault on the Mafia, which went into hyper mode when he served as JFK's Attorney General. He may have continued JFK's quest to dismantle the CIA. He wanted to see LBJ sent to prison for atrocities and murders LBJ had been involved in for decades. Above all, this cabal was terrified at the prospect of Bobby creating an organization to look into his Brother's death. They knew that any true, unbiased search for the truth would come back to haunt them. Indeed, an assassination attempt on Jimmy Carter (which most of the American public have no knowledge of) was a clear message from the CIA to Carter to stay away from any investigation into JFK's death.

This is the America we live in today, and our forefathers who created this country and our Constitution are no doubt spinning in their graves. They envisioned a land where politicians worked for the people instead of themselves, where political parties would work together for the good of the American people, where Government power was limited instead of onerous, elitist, controlling, pervasive and dedicated above all else to their own agendas.

We still have time to restore America back to the dream these brilliant, prescient men imagined we should and could be so many years ago. But until we bring this cabal to its knees they will continue to flourish, and it's only a matter of time until they remove the next threat to their evil campaign to subjugate us all to their master plan of complete domination. I live for the day someone, somehow is able to render them powerless.

The souls of JFK, RFK, MLK, Malcolm X and countless others deserve no less.

Tim Brennan May, 2023

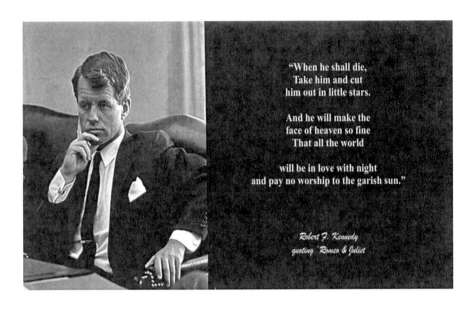

"When he shall die,
Take him and cut
him out in little stars.

And he will make the
face of heaven so fine
That all the world

will be in love with night
and pay no worship to the garish sun."

Robert F. Kennedy
quoting "Romeo & Juliet"

Two

<u>Death of A President</u>

November 22, 1963 began as most days for Robert Kennedy. Two days earlier the JFK and RFK families had gathered to celebrate Robert's 38th birthday. On the morning of the 21st, at 9:45 a.m., President and Mrs. Kennedy boarded Marine One for the short flight to Andrews Air Force Base before embarking on their flight to Texas to campaign for the 1964 election.

Robert F. Kennedy, the U.S. Attorney General at the time, had spent the morning of November 22, 1963, at a Justice Department conference on fighting against organized crime. Afterwards, he invited U.S. Attorney Robert Morgenthau and his press secretary, Ed Guthman back to his estate at Hickory Hill, in McLean, VA., Hickory Hill. The group was enjoying a poolside lunch when Ethel informed Bobby at 1:45 p.m. that he had a phone call from FBI Director, J. Edgar Hoover. Hoover said, "I have news for you," his voice devoid of emotion. "The President's been shot. It may be fatal." Robert was completely devastated and was comforted by his wife, Ethel. A few moments later, the phone rang again. Bobby simply answered, "Yes." Hoover replied, "The President is dead" and simply hung up the phone. Years later Bobby would remark that he felt Hoover enjoyed sharing this news with a man who was born after Hoover became Director of the FBI and who now was having to answer to the Kennedy brothers, especially Bobby. He said to Guthman, "there's so much bitterness. I thought they'd get one of us.

RFK being comforted by his children at Hickory Hill residence.

I just always thought it would be me." Within minutes of the announcement of JFK's death, Hickory Hill was surrounded by federal marshals and Secret Service agents fearing that JFK's murder might possibly be part of a larger conspiracy. Ironically, Secret Service agents were never assigned to protect a Presidential candidate until 1968 when Robert Kennedy was killed while running for President. Within an hour, Bobby called CIA headquarters in Langley, just two miles down Dolley Madison Boulevard. After reaching a high-level official at the CIA, Bobby said, "Did your outfit have anything to do with this horror?" The official refused to answer, and Bobby informed them to have Director John McCone summoned to his house immediately. When McCone arrived, Bobby confronted him again with this question. McCone denied any CIA involvement. According to author David Talbot's 2007 book, 'Brothers—The Hidden History of the Kennedy Years,' Bobby Kennedy knew that McCone, a wealthy Republican businessman from California with no intelligence background, did not have a firm grasp on all aspects of the agency's work. Real control over the clandestine service revolved around the Number two man, Richard Helms, the shrewd bureaucrat whose intelligence career went back to the agency's OSS origins in World War II. "It was clear that McCone was out of the loop—Dick Helms was running the agency," recently commented RFK aide John Seigenthaler, another crusading newspaper reporter, like Guthman, whom Bobby had recruited for his Justice Department team. "Anything McCone found out was by accident." (a)

John McCone   Richard Helms

Bobby then called Enrique "Harry" Ruiz-Williams, a Bay of Pigs veteran who was his most trusted ally among exiled political leaders. Bobby said point-blank, "One of your guys did it." By this time, Oswald had been arrested in Dallas. Recently released documents suggest that Bobby Kennedy had heard the name Lee

Harvey Oswald and had connected him with the CIA's war on Castro. When Oswald was arrested in Dallas, Bobby apparently realized that the CIA's clandestine activities against Fidel Castro had been redirected at his brother.

Within two hours of the assassination, Bobby was already looking into the CIA's possible involvement. He was also looking at the Mafia. Since becoming Attorney General, Bobby and JFK were aggressively prosecuting Mafia chieftains. One year prior, an FBI informant had informed Walter Sheridan that Jimmy Hoffa had said, "I've got to do something about that Son of a Bitch Bobby Kennedy. He's got to go." At the time of the assassination, mob leader and Hoffa associate Carlos Marcello was on trial in New Orleans for 'conspiracy to defraud the United States government by obtaining a false Guatemalan birth certificate' and 'conspiracy to obstruct the United States government in the exercise of its right to deport Carlos Marcello.' This was the culmination of a three-year effort by the Attorney General to get Marcello out of the country. Marcello was acquitted of all charges that same day, November 22, 1963. In his book, 'Mob Lawyer,' Frank Ragano states how Hoffa had instructed him in the summer of 1963 to tell Trafficante and Marcello that it was time to kill the President. Ragano says he thought, "Hoffa was only 'joking' but the mobsters seemed to take it much more seriously." (b)

At 4:20 p.m., EST, Air Force One was headed to Washington D.C. with JFK's remains aboard. Bobby Kennedy had already been ridiculed by new President Johnson placing calls to the Justice Department after the assassination to get the 'exact wording' of the oath of office of President. Aboard Air Force One, Sergeant Ayres, made telephone contact with Rose Kennedy through the switchboard routed through the White House. The content of the phone call is printed below:

LBJ: "Mrs. Kennedy?"

Rose: "Yes, Yes, Mr. President. Yes"

LBJ: "I wish to God there was something that I could do, and I wanted to tell you that we are grieving with you."

Rose: "Yes, well thank you very much."

LBJ: "Here's Lady Bird."

Rose: "Thank you very much, I know you loved Jack, and he loved you—"

Lady: "Mrs. Kennedy, we feel like we've just had-"

Rose: "Yes, all right."

Lady: "—we are glad that the nation had your son—"

Rose: "Yes, yes"

Lady: "—as long as it did."

Rose: "Yes, well, thank you, Lady Bird. Thank you very much. Goodbye."

Lady: "Love and prayers to all of you."

Rose: "Yes. Thank you very much. Goodbye. Goodbye."

     Air Force One landed in Washington at 6:05 p.m. Robert Kennedy was already there waiting alone in the back of an Army truck. After the stairs were wheeled into place he rushed into the plane's front entrance, pushed his way past LBJ without even acknowledging him, looking for Jackie. "Where's Jackie?" Bobby said, "I want to be with Jackie." Kenny O'Donnell and the rest of the Secret Service agents surrounded the casket as Bobby hugged Jackie. "Hi, Jackie," Bobby said, "I'm here." Jackie cried and fell into Bobby's arms, "Oh Bobby," she said. Kenny

JFK's casket being removed at Andrews Air Force Base.

O'Donnell stated, "We carried it (casket) on the plane, we're going to carry it off the plane." The JFK Honor Guard was in place to remove the body from the plane, but the Secret Service demanded that they remove the President's body from Air Force

One and took control of the ambulance which would take his body to Bethesda for the autopsy.

JFK Honor Guard, Hubert Clark (U.S. Navy) was one of the original six members assigned to transport the body of their Commander in Chief from Andrews Air Force Base to Bethesda. According to Hubert, "we were ambushed by men in civilian suits." The Secret Service also removed the Navy ambulance personnel, and agents Greer and Kellerman (who were both in the President's limousine during the motorcade in Dallas) delivered the body of the President to Bethesda Naval Hospital, with Jackie and Bobby accompanying the body to autopsy.

Hubert Clark and the five other remaining Honor Guard members were ordered by Lt. Byrd into an awaiting helicopter to shadow the ambulance from Andrews to Bethesda. Moments before the ambulance arrived, the helicopter flew ahead and landed at Bethesda. The Honor Guard was ordered into the flatbed of a pickup truck to be delivered to the morgue dock. Lt. Byrd said, "We will not remove the remains of the President until Jackie and Bobby go inside." The Honor Guard was awaiting at the morgue dock when the gray Navy ambulance began backing up to the dock. Hubert stated, "Then all of a sudden, the ambulance just took off." Lt. Byrd ordered the Honor Guard back into the flatbed truck and they began to chase the ambulance around the grounds of Bethesda. "We were following the ambulance closely because the driver of the truck knew the grounds of Bethesda very well. Then all of a sudden, the ambulance turned their lights out, and we lost it, for like ten minutes," said Hubert. He continued, "we searched the grounds and passed the morgue dock twice before finally finding the ambulance parked there on our third pass, with Godfrey McHugh standing at the dock."

The Honor Guard removed the body of the President and placed the remains into the anteroom of the morgue to await Dennis David's team to take the body into the morgue. Lt. Byrd ordered the six men of the Honor Guard to protect the morgue entrance, anteroom entrance and entrance into the hospital from the morgue dock. Nobody was allowed to enter. The Honor Guard stood watch the entire time the autopsy was being performed.

Honor Guard member in distance on right.

JFK's autopsy was a complete travesty. The three physicians chosen to perform the autopsy of the century had never performed an autopsy involving criminal gunshot wounds. Dr. Humes, Finck and Boswell were career Naval men just a few

JFK Autopsy physicians: Boswell, Humes & Finck.

years short of retirement and were being directed by others at the autopsy. Technician Paul O'Connor described the autopsy, "we'd be doing a procedure and all of a sudden a Doctor (pathologist) would disappear for a moment and come back and say we needed to move onto another part of the autopsy." He continued, "the entire autopsy was controlled and there was no flow of normal procedure." (c). More information regarding the autopsy is available in the books, 'Best Evidence' by David Lifton and 'The Innocence of Oswald' by Gary Fannin and Tim Brennan.

The body of the President was prepared by Tom Robinson of Gawler's Funeral Home in D.C. Robinson admitted, "we had to use more pancake (mortician makeup) to cover the cheek and neck of the President as there was glass shards causing the embalming fluid to disseminate." (d) The body of the President finally arrived back to the White House at approximately 4:30 a.m., November 23, 1963, less than 48 hours after leaving for Texas.

Honor Guard carrying JFK's casket towards the White House East Room.

Once JFK's body was returned to the White House East Room, Bobby and Jackie discussed the plans for JFK's funeral. There was a question as to whether to leave the casket open or not. Bobby asked his friend and advisor, Charles Spalding, along with Robert McNamara, to go view the body in the East Room of the White House. "We both decided it would be better if it weren't open," said Spalding. He continued, "McNamara concurred, and other people must have concurred. My recollection is that Arthur Schlesinger was there at the same time." Spalding continued, "I remember going upstairs with him and Mrs. Kennedy and Jackie's mother was there. A terrible sense of loss overwhelmed everybody who was present in the room, and Bobby was trying to calm everybody and get them to bed. But it had been a terrible, terrible day, and at that period of time—time seems to be rushing along in moments like that. It was a terrible day, and he had been through the most awful experience, and he was trying to get everybody in their rooms and try to get them to bed, preparing them for the next day. So, he asked me to come down to his room."

Bobby slept in the Lincoln Bedroom that night. So, I said, "Listen, you ought to take a sleeping pill, because he was terribly distraught but in control of himself while I was there. So, I went to look for a sleeping pill and came back—found one some place and got it—and gave it to him and closed the door as he was." All the time he had been under control. Then, I just heard him sobbing. He was saying, "Why, God? Why, God, why?" Before I closed the door of the Lincoln Bedroom on him, Bobby said to me in such a calm, quiet voice, "It's such an awful shame, the country was going so well. We really had it going." Spalding continued to say, "when I heard the door close, I just heard him—he just gave way completely, and he was just racked with sobs and the only person he could address himself to was, "Why, God, why? What possible reason could there be in this?" He continued, "I think at that terrible moment—and it's a terrible testing of everything, probably all the things he thought—it was so incredibly unjust to him to have that happen at that particular time after everything had been. I mean, just the terrible injustice of it, the senselessness of it all hit him, and he just collapsed, and collapsed in that he sobbed by himself in the night and slept." (e)

JFK entering the East Room for the last time, November 23, 1963.

Both Bobby and Jackie knew immediately that Lee Oswald had not assassinated John F. Kennedy. This would be confirmed on Sunday when Jack Ruby silenced Oswald forever. Bobby and Jackie had already decided to privately communicate to Khrushchev and the Soviet Union that they did not believe Lee Oswald was the assassin and that the current administration might promote the theory of Soviet involvement to deflect from any domestic involvement. According to Peter Lawford, Jackie and Bobby wanted the Soviet leadership to know that despite

Oswald's connections to the Communist world, the Kennedy's believed that the President was killed by a domestic conspiracy.(f)

Publicly, Jackie and Bobby endorsed the Warren Commission's conclusion that Oswald acted alone. In their 1998 book, 'One Hell of a Gamble: Khrushchev, Castro and Kennedy, 1958-1964,' authors Aleksandr Fusenko and Timothy Naftali reported that when Jacqueline Kennedy's artist friend William Walton traveled to Moscow on a previously scheduled trip a week after President Kennedy's assassination, Walton carried the above "felled by domestic opponents" message from Jackie and Bobby to another friend of the Kennedy administration, Georgi Bolshakov, a Russian diplomat. Bolshakov had served as a back-channel link between the White House and the Kremlin during the Cuban Missile Crisis in October 1962. (g)

Jackie Kennedy with William Walton.

In the weeks that followed his brother's death, Bobby was a shattered man, physically in pain for the loss of his brother. He was suffering from 'survivor guilt,' wondering why he was alive since he considered himself to have a ruthless reputation. In the years that followed, Bobby began quoting Jack in his speeches. Nobody noticed this more than his brother-in-law, Peter Lawford. On the weekend of JFK's funeral, Lawford was present in the White House when Bobby told family members that JFK had been killed by a powerful plot that grew out of one of the CIA's secret anti-Castro operations. "There was nothing we could do at this point," Bobby said, "since they were facing a formidable enemy and they no longer controlled the government." Justice would have to wait until Bobby could regain the White House in 1968.

As Attorney General it was still Bobby's responsibility to enforce the laws of the nation. Now, however, he was having to take orders from J. Edgar Hoover instead of the other way around. Although RFK was technically Hoover's boss, he would have to listen to Hoover's opinion more than before because the Director had the ear of the President, Lyndon Baines Johnson. LBJ and Hoover were neighbors in D.C. for years before Johnson ascended to the Vice Presidency and then became President. Now Bobby had to take orders from LBJ, the man who occupied his brother's chair in the oval office.

RFK and LBJ despised each other. This was obvious from the moment that JFK offered the Vice Presidency to LBJ as a sign of respect for him being runner-up at the Democratic National Convention in 1960. When LBJ accepted, Bobby was furious and asked JFK to rescind the offer. JFK refused. Bobby would take matters into his own hands and personally went to the Johnson suite and told LBJ to decline the Vice President position. LBJ also declined, but he did call JFK to make sure the position was still

RFK (L) with LBJ in the oval office.

available. Now, the tables were turned, and Bobby was taking orders from a man that he never trusted or respected.

The only saving grace for Bobby was in the fact that he knew LBJ needed to build upon JFK's legacy and pass the Civil Rights bill before the 1964 election. LBJ had yet to name a Vice Presidential candidate in 1964 and many wanted Bobby on the ticket with LBJ. Even family insiders were urging Bobby to agree, since LBJ was 56 years old and was not a healthy individual. He was known to drink and smoke profusely and had already had a heart attack. Some felt this would be the quickest path to the White House for Bobby since they did not believe LBJ would survive a complete term. Of course, LBJ had no intentions of putting RFK on the 1964 ticket. He knew that RFK was too powerful to play second fiddle to him in the oval office. This was never more symbolic than at the 1964 Democratic Convention in

LBJ signs Civil Rights Act of 1964 with Martin Luther King present.

Atlantic City. Anticipating that Bobby would receive an emotional reaction from the delegation ten months after his brother's death, LBJ asked Bobby to speak on the final night after his own nomination speech and after Hubert Humphrey was securely nominated as Vice President-Elect. The reaction of the crowd was overwhelming. A 22-minute ovation from the crowd culminated in Bobby being introduced to speak. Although it would take an additional four years and a limited term in the Senate, Bobby was in control of his destiny, the White House in 1968, and whether he would run against LBJ or not. LBJ was enormously relieved when Bobby decided to leave his administration and run for the Senate seat from New York. LBJ actually campaigned for Bobby, knowing that he would gain another important seat in the Senate.

Publicly, Bobby and Jackie would endorse the Warren Report and its lone gunman theory. Privately, Bobby said the report was nothing more than a public relations exercise designed to reassure the public, and personally called the investigation, "a shoddy report devoid of truth." Privately, he was continuing to investigate his brother's death and was planning to reopen the case if he ever won the White House. He held onto medical evidence from his brother's autopsy, including JFK's brain and tissue samples. The brain and tissue samples were believed to have been buried with JFK on his exhumation. In Robert Groden's book, 'Absolute Proof,' there are photographs with Robert, Edward and Cardinal Cushing standing at the head of the grave with a small box containing President Kennedy's brain beside Robert's feet. This box was also seen when cemetery staff dug the grave for Jacqueline Kennedy Onassis' funeral in May, 1994. Some researchers suggested the box was Bobby's way of protecting his brother's image because of all the prescription medication JFK was on for his back pain and Addison's disease.

Ted and Robert Kennedy at 1967 exhumation of JFK to install permanent gas line for eternal flame.

Edward and Robert overseeing JFK's exhumation. Note box on right.

Final blessing before box with JFK's brain is placed inside burial plot.

After Jim Garrison arrested Clay Shaw in March 1967, Bobby sent Walter Sheridan to New Orleans to check into the investigation. Sheridan was working with NBC News at the time and was probably already being paid by the CIA under their Operation Mockingbird clandestine operations. Sheridan told RFK that Garrison was a fraud. Bobby had no way of knowing that the CIA had infiltrated the news media and were essentially writing the news for television. After Sheridan went to New Orleans, Bobby began relying more on his press secretary, Frank Mankiewicz to gather information about the assassination and the investigations into his brother's death in case there ever was another formal investigation. Mankiewicz's own conclusions were that rogue CIA agents had probably killed JFK in retaliation for not providing air cover for the Bay of Pigs invasion. Bobby would always deflect serious researchers such as Mark Lane and Sylvia Meagher who wanted his viewpoint on his brother's assassination. He was privately continuing his own investigation for the purpose of reopening the case if and when he won the White House. The only researcher he did meet with at his Senate office was Penn Jones Jr., a small-town publisher of the Midlothian Mirror in Midlothian, Texas. Jones would go on to write a series of books on the JFK assassination titled, "Forgive My Grief."

Just as Richard Nixon knew that the 1960 election was probably stolen from him in Illinois and West Virginia, Bobby knew the Senate was a small step out of the shadows of LBJ's administration. Bobby used his time in the Senate to slowly emerge from his grief for his fallen brother. As historian Ronald Steel said, "Only gradually and partially did he (RFK) emerge from his grief. It left a melancholy that could be seen in his eyes, and it tempered his arrogance and impatience. Grief helped humanize him. It pulled him into the world of human imperfection and suffering. It even made him more tolerant. And it forced him, bit by bit, to begin the effort to reevaluate a life based on power, will, and the drive to conquer. It was during these months that the 'new Bobby' is said to have emerged from the chrysalis of the old," Steel continues, "This is where the legend of John Kennedy leaves off and the legend of Robert Kennedy begins." (h)

Bobby knew he must wait for the proper moment to mount a comeback for the Kennedy dynasty at 1600 Pennsylvania Avenue.

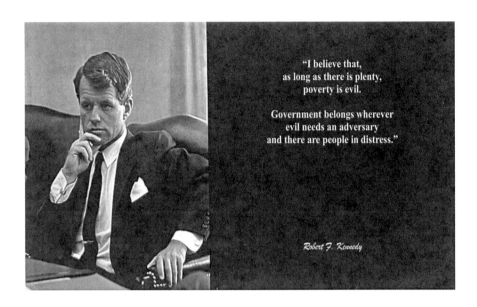

"I believe that,
as long as there is plenty,
poverty is evil.

Government belongs wherever
evil needs an adversary
and there are people in distress."

Robert F. Kennedy

Three

<u>Senator From New York</u>

On August 25, 1964 at the Gracie Mansion in New York City Attorney General Robert F. Kennedy announced his candidacy to represent the state of New York in the U.S. Senate. The speech in which he declared his candidacy is reprinted below:

"I have decided to make myself available for the nomination of the Democratic State Convention. I have made that decision because I think our country faces a fundamental political choice. Our traditional aspirations for peace and prosperity, justice, and decency, are being questioned. All that President Kennedy stood for, and all that President Johnson is trying to accomplish, all the progress that has been made, is threatened by a new and dangerous Republican assault. No one associated with President Kennedy and with President Johnson—no one committed to participating in public life—can sit on the sidelines with so much at stake. In this struggle, New York has a special role to play, a role which transcends the question of electoral votes for the Presidency. For New York is the supreme testing ground for the most acute national problems of our time—the problems of racial harmony, of employment, of youth, of education, and of the quality of urban and suburban life."

Robert Kennedy would have to confront his biggest obstacle, the fact that he was from Massachusetts and had only recently purchased a house in New York. By claiming loyalty to New York, he informed the media that his parents had owned a house in New York since 1926 and that he had spent six years at school in the state. Bobby was uniquely qualified in the fact that he had managed JFK's Senate and Presidential campaigns and had gained a reputation for tough political infighting and loyalty.

New York Times, August 23, 1964.

Kennedy would be competing against Republican incumbent, Kenneth Keating. The New York Times printed the article two days before Robert officially announced his candidacy. It is reprinted here:

WASHINGTON, Aug. 22—The impending contest between Senator Kenneth B. Keating of New York and Robert F. Kennedy, soon to be of New York, seems certain to present an interesting study in contrasts.

Senator Keating is 64 years old, white-haired, ruddy of complexion and inclined to be a little stocky. Mr. Kennedy is 38, boyish and slender, with a shock of sandy hair reminiscent of his late brother's unruly forelock.

Over the last 18 years, Senator Keating has won seven elections, six for the House and one for the Senate, and has never been defeated. In his 13 years in public life, Mr. Kennedy has never run for office himself although he has extensive experience as a campaign manager.

Senator Keating has lived in New York State all his life and has been campaigning for reelection through its cities and villages for nearly six years now, ever since his first Senate contest resulted in a 135,000-vote majority that was too close for comfort.

Mr. Kennedy, although he has lived in New York City at various times, has his legal residence in Massachusetts and his home in the Virginia suburbs of Washington.

And yet, despite all these sharp contrasts between the two men, many observers now believe that their

competition for the Senate will reveal few basic differences in principle between the candidates.

Senator Keating has firmly ensconced himself in the liberal wing of the Republican party, a position that is sometimes difficult for the politically uninitiated to distinguish from the liberal wing of the Democratic party.

Mr. Kennedy can safely be expected to run, implicitly if not explicitly, on the philosophy and programs of the New Frontier advanced by his late brother. This is not likely to place him in serious conflict with his Republican opponent over many issues.

For example, it appears remote indeed that any civil rights issue will be involved directly in the New York Senate campaign. From their past statements, the two candidates stand shoulder to shoulder on the question of equal opportunity and the Government's responsibility to insure it.

There is at least some possibility, however, that Senator Keating might fall heir to support from white voters who fear the advent of Negroes in their schools, their neighborhoods, and their society; such voting would probably be more of a protest against Mr. Kennedy's role in the civil rights struggle as Attorney General than an endorsement of Mr. Keating.

Mr. Keating said when he announced his candidacy this week that he wanted no part of any such "white backlash" votes, but this may not sway those who are anxious to register a protest at the polls.

With the campaign not even officially under way — nominations will be made on Aug, 31 and Sept. 1 — the major issue other than the personalities of the two contenders seems likely to be the Republican argument that Mr. Kennedy is a "carpetbagger," an outsider moving into New York purely to advance his own political interests.

Although it is not the easiest issue in politics to explain, Mr. Kennedy may be able to get some mileage out of reapportionment. As Attorney General, he threw the weight of the Justice Department behind the "one man, one vote" concept adopted by the Supreme Court that will require considerable redrafting of legislative district lines.

Senator Keating may be caught in the middle on the issue. Most New York Republicans have opposed legislative reapportionment in the state; it would almost certainly weaken their party's hold on the Legislature. But the Democrats and independents to whom Mr. Keating must look, for support are inclined to favor reapportionment.

Purely as a matter of figures, Mr. Kennedy would seem to enjoy a distinct advantage. The registration of the Democratic and Liberal parties combined exceeds the number of enrolled Republicans by about 500,000. A Conservative party candidate could drain off 150,000 votes that would otherwise be Republican.

But such figures are deceptive. Although John F. Kennedy carried New York State in 1960 by 385,000 votes, Nelson Rockefeller swept in by more than 500,000 votes in both 1958 and 1962 and his Republican running mate the latter year, Senator Jacob K. Javits, ran up a margin of nearly a million votes.

As a liberal Republican, Senator Keating can reasonably expect to attract a good share of these Rockefeller-Javits supporters. But the key question is how much the presence of a conservative, Senator Barry Goldwater, at the top of the ticket is likely to discourage such a voting trend.

Mr. Kennedy faces two related questions: Can he profit from the strength that most observers now expect Lyndon Johnson to show in New York State, and will he be able to recapture the large numbers of otherwise Republican voters of the Roman Catholic faith who supported his brother four years ago?

Mr. Kennedy's chief asset as he goes into the campaign is the close public association between himself and his brother and the great wave of common affection and sympathy aroused by the assassination for all the Kennedy family, which is clearly not yet spent.

Senator Keating's strongest points are his familiarity with the state, his liberal record and, perhaps critically, the fact that he will offer an acceptable alternative to almost any voter except a rabid conservative who is dismayed or disturbed by Mr. Kennedy's candidacy.

One question still unresolved is whether the two Senate candidates will present a marked contrast as campaigners. Mr. Keating is a skilled professional of the handshaking, sidewalk tour school. He reads speech texts well and has earned a reputation as a political wit.

Mr. Kennedy, on the other hand, tends to be painfully shy, with almost a plaintive quality, in public. He is not inclined to be comfortable reading a printed speech text, but he can project a sympathetic intensity extemporaneously when he speaks for a cause in which he believes.

A close personal and political associate of the Kennedy family, expressing confidence in Robert Kennedy's potential as a campaigner, observed recently: "You should have seen his brother when he started out."

Keating would accuse Kennedy of being a 'carpetbagger' and using the state of New York as nothing but a steppingstone to advance his political aspirations. Despite being correct, Keating's comment was viewed as a candidate expecting to win based upon longevity. RFK, like his brother before him, used television to challenge his opponent by saying, "If the Senator of the state of New York is going to be selected on who's lived here the longest, then I think people are going to vote for my opponent. If it's going to be selected on who's got the best New York accent, then I think I'm probably out too. But I think if it's going to be selected on the basis of who can make the best United States Senator, I think I'm still in the contest."

RFK won the Senate seat primarily due to LBJ's landslide victory for re-election as President. RFK won the popular vote by a margin of 3,823,749 to Keating's 3,104,056, or 53.5% to 43.4% (primarily due to LBJ's dominance in New York. LBJ would garner nearly 1.1 million more votes than RFK.) Akin to current voting, Democrats tend to dominate in urban areas while Republicans tend to receive the rural vote. The break down by county is listed below.

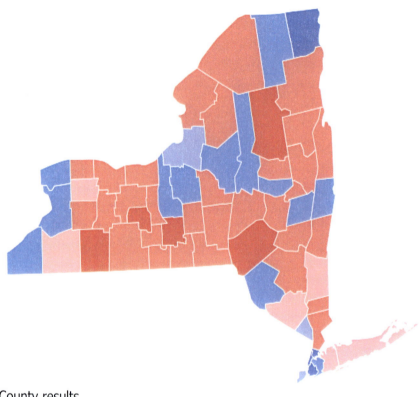

County results
Kennedy: 40–50%   50–60%   60–70%
Keating: 40–50%   50–60%   60–70% (a)

RFK immediately became involved with gun control. With the assassination of his brother fresh on his mind, Bobby reached out to Senator Thomas J. Dodd (Dem., CT) who had introduced S.1975, a gun control measure the previous year based upon a 2½ year investigation by the Senate Judiciary's Juvenile Delinquency Subcommittee. The proposal was not enacted. With RFK's help Senator Dodd then introduced S.1592, a bill to amend the Federal Firearms Act on March 22, 1965, subsequently co-sponsored by Robert Kennedy in May 1965. The proposed legislation was designed to accomplish the following:

First: It would prohibit the shipment of firearms in interstate commerce, except between federally licensed manufacturers, dealers, and importers. This provision would have the effect of prohibiting the so-called mail-order traffic in firearms to unlicensed persons. It would leave to each state the responsibility and authority for control ling the sale and disposition of firearms within its borders. There are several important exceptions to this general prohibition against interstate shipment. Sportsmen could continue to take their shotguns or rifles across state lines. Pistols could be carried in interstate commerce but only for a lawful purpose and only in conformity with state laws. Further, firearms could be shipped to a licensee for service and return to the sender. However, a non-licensee could no longer buy weapons from out-of-state mail order dealers. Sales would be made by retail dealers and would thus be subject to record-keeping requirements. These records would then have new meaning; they would not be rendered futile by an unrecorded flow of mail-order guns.

Second: Licensed retail dealers would be required to limit sales of handguns to residents of their state who are 21 years of age or older; they would be prohibited from selling any firearm to a person under the age of 18. In accordance with regulations to be prescribed by the Secretary of the Treasury, licensed dealers would be required to ascertain the identity and place of residence of a purchaser. Further, it would be unlawful for a dealer

to sell a firearm to any person when he knows or has reasonable cause to believe that such person is under indictment for or has been convicted of a felony or is a fugitive from justice. These provisions of the proposed legislation do not address themselves to the question of permits to possess or to use firearms, leaving it to the states and local com munities to decide what they need and want in that regard. Thus, for example, while the bill limits the sale of shotguns and rifles to persons who are at least 18 years of age, it does not preclude such persons from using guns if such use is permitted by state or local law.

Third: The bill would raise the annual license fees for a dealer from the present token of $1.00 to $100. It would also establish a license fee of $250 for a pawnbroker who deals in firearms. Specific standards are established under which an application for a license shall be disapproved, after notice and opportunity for a hearing. The purpose of this provision of the proposed legislation is to limit the issuance of licenses to bona fide dealers. Under existing law, anyone other than a felon can, upon the mere allegation that he is a dealer and the payment of a fee of $1.00, demand and obtain a license. According to the Secretary of the Treasury, some 50 or 60 thousand people have done this, some of them merely to put themselves in a position to obtain personal guns at wholesale. There would be nothing to prevent them from obtaining licenses in order to ship or receive concealable weapons through the mails, or to circumvent state or local requirements.

Fourth: The bill would permit the Secretary of the Treasury to curb the flow into the United States of surplus military weapons and other firearms not suitable for sporting purposes. However, weapons imported for science, research, or military training, or as antiques and curios, could be allowed.

Fifth: The importation and interstate shipment of large caliber weapons, such as bazookas and antitank guns, and other destructive devices would be brought under effective federal control.

Congressional Record of S.1592 (eventually Gun Control Act of 1968).

Speaking in support of the bill, Robert Kennedy said, "For too long we dealt with these deadly weapons as if they were harmless toys. Yet their very presence, the ease of their acquisition and the familiarity of their appearance have let to thousands of deaths each year. With the passage of this bill, we will begin to meet our responsibilities. It would save hundreds of thousands of lives in this country and spare thousands of family's grief and heartache." In May 1968, during a campaign stop in Roseburg, Oregon while running for President, he would also add, "keeping firearms away from people who have no business with guns or rifles. The bill forbade mail order sale of guns to the very young, those with criminal records and the insane." Unfortunately, none of this came to fruition until after his own assassination.

True to the present day, the principal objections to the proposed legislation would come from the National Rifle Association and its members. Attorney General Nicholas Katzenbach issued the following statements regarding the position of the NRA.

"This measure is not intended to curtail the ownership of guns among those legally entitled to own them. It is not intended to deprive people of guns used either for sport or for self-protection. It is not intended to force regulation on unwilling states.

The purpose of this measure is simple: it is, merely, to help the states protect themselves against the unchecked flood of mail-order weapons to residents whose purposes might not be responsible, or even lawful. S.1592 would provide such assistance to the extent that the states and the people of the states want it.

There is demonstrable need for regulation of the interstate mail order sale of guns. This bill is a response to that need. It was carefully drafted; it is receiving detailed attention from this Subcommittee.

But, nevertheless, S1592 now has itself become a target for the verbal fire of the National Rifle Association and others who represent hunters and sporting shooters. These opponents feel their views most deeply, as is evident from the bitterness and volume of their opposition. It is no secret to any member of Congress that the NRA sent out a mailing of 700,000 letters to its membership urging a barrage of mail to Senators and Congressmen.

There is no question that the views of the NRA should be heard and given full weight. There is no question that so many people with an interest in gun legislation should have every opportunity to express it. But those views also need to be evaluated and thus I would like now to turn to analysis of the opposition arguments.

It has been suggested, for example, by Franklin Orth, executive vice president of the NRA, that S.1592 gives the Secretary of the Treasury 'unlimited power to surround all sales of guns by dealers with arbitrary and burdensome regulations and restrictions.'

I fear this is an exaggeration flowing from the heat of opposition. The Secretary's regulations must be reasonable. I should think that the reasonableness of the regulations promulgated by the Secretary of the Treasury under the existing provisions of the Federal Firearms Act would contradict the assumption of 'burdensome regulations.'

Further, the Administrative Procedure Act assures all interested parties of an opportunity to be heard before the issuance of substantive rules and regulations. The NRA and other gun interests have, in the past, taken full advantage of this opportunity and clearly could do so in the future. And still further, the regulations are subject to review and reversal by the courts and by Congress should they be felt arbitrary and capricious.

It has also been suggested that S.1592 requires anyone engaged in the manufacture of ammunition to pay $1,000 for a manufacturer's license. The bill does not do so. It does not cover shotgun ammunition at all, and the license fee for manufacturers of other types of ammunition is $500.

It is true that anyone selling rifle ammunition, even .22 caliber, would be compelled to have a $100 dealer license. Why shouldn't he? He is dealing ammunition for a lethal weapon. The many dealers in ammunition who also sell firearms would not, however, be required to pay an additional ammunition fee. Nor is there anything in the legislation that would, as has been stated, require a club engaged in reloading for its members to obtain a manufacturer's license.

A further specific objection raised against this measure is that it would forbid a dealer to sell to a non-resident of his state. The objection is stated in a misleading way. The bill does forbid such sales of handguns, but it specifically excepts weapons like rifles and shotguns most commonly used by sportsmen and least commonly used by criminals.

A similar objection is made on the grounds that the measure would prohibit all mail-order sales of firearms to individuals. While this is an accurate description of the measure with respect to interstate and foreign commerce, the bill would not foreclose now allowable shipments within a state. Any control of such commerce is left to the states. One last comment on the specific NRA objections, as expressed in the letter sent to its membership. The letter described this measure as one which conceivably could lead to the elimination of 'the private ownership of all guns.' I am compelled to say that this is not conceivable. I am compelled to say that there is only one word which can serve in reply to such a fear – preposterous.

More generally, I really cannot understand why the legislation we are talking about should seem a threat at all to sportsmen, hunters, farmers, and others who have a productive or necessary or enjoy able interest in the use of rifles, shotguns, or sporting handguns. Nothing that we propose here could intelligently be construed as impairing the enjoyment they derive from shooting.

This legislation would, indeed, make some changes in the distribution of firearms. It would, indeed, by outlawing mail-order sales of firearms between states, bring about changes in the commercial firearms world. It would, indeed, challenge interests which have thrived on the present state of unregulated chaos. But such a challenge is tragically overdue.

Which is more significant, the right not to be slightly inconvenienced in the purchase of a firearm, or the right not to be terrorized, robbed, wounded, or killed?

As the chief law enforcement officer of the United States, I come before you today to ask you to supply the only conceivable answer to that question. I come, with all the urgency at my command, to ask the Subcommittee to report this measure favorably and to ask the Congress to enact it without delay." (b)

Although S.1592 did not initially pass, it did bring about changes to gun laws. The Gun Control Act of 1968 was signed into law on October 22, 1968, banning mail order sales of rifles and shotguns and prohibiting most felons, drug users and people found mentally incompetent. Ironically, this bill was signed by none other than Lyndon Baines Johnson, the man who benefited the most from a mail-order rifle, if you believe the Lee Oswald lone gunman theory. It was also signed into law after the assassinations of Medgar Evers, Malcolm X, JFK, Dr. Martin Luther King and the co-sponsor, Robert Francis Kennedy. The Gun Control Act of 1968 was amended in 1993 by the Brady Handgun Violence Prevention Act. This amendment was in response to James Brady being critically injured on March 30, 1981 during the Reagan assassination attempt. The amendment introduced a background check requirement of prospective gun purchasers by licensed sellers, and created a list of categories of individuals to whom the sale of firearms is prohibited.

Robert Kennedy was involved in the passage of numerous laws during his brief time as Senator from New York. These include the following:

The Civil Rights Act of 1964—prohibits discrimination on the basis of race, color, religion, sex, or national origin. Provisions of this civil rights act forbade discrimination on the basis of sex, as well as race in hiring, promoting, and firing.

Medicare and Medicaid Act of 1965—also known as the Social Security Amendments of 1965. It established Medicare, a health insurance program for the elderly, and Medicaid, a health insurance program for people with limited income.

The Voting Rights Act of 1965—aimed to overcome legal barriers at the state and local levels that prevented African Americans from exercising their right to vote as guaranteed under the 15th Amendment to the U.S. Constitution.

Freedom of Information Act of 1966—also known as FOIA, generally provides any person with the statutory right, enforceable in court, to obtain access to government information in executive branch agency records.

The Highway Safety Act of 1966—authorized Federal funds for distribution to the states, with a requirement that each state implement a highway safety program by December 31, 1968 or suffer a 10% reduction in Federally-apportioned funds.

The Age Discrimination in Employment Act 1967—protects certain applicants and employees 40 years of age and older from discrimination on the basis of age in hiring, promotion, discharge, compensation, or terms, conditions, or privileges of employment.

Public Broadcasting Act of 1967—details the costs of upgrading educational broadcasting, both for radio and television, as well as establishing how much of the money budgeted to educational broadcasting can be granted to broadcasters in each state and how that granted money is used.

Fair Housing Act of 1968—This act expanded on previous acts and prohibited discrimination concerning the sale, rental, and financing of housing based on race, religion, national origin, sex, handicap, and family status.

Robert Kennedy championed civil rights and social justice issues while Senator. He traveled to the Mississippi Delta, Appalachia, migrant workers' camps and urban ghettos to study the effects of poverty, and made trips abroad to apartheid-ruled South Africa to advocate for the advancement and equality of human rights.

RFK in Mississippi Delta.

Robert F. Kennedy's address in South Africa is considered as his greatest speech and was called *"the most stirring and memorable address ever to come from a foreigner in South Africa".* This *"most important speech"* was inspirational for a great many anti-Apartheid activists including Nelson Mandela who was imprisoned at that time. Kennedy delivered the speech at the University of Cape Town on June 6, 1966, the University's "Day of Reaffirmation of Academic and Human Freedom." South Africa was not amused. Forty news correspondents who were supposed to cover the event were denied visas, although after some hesitation Kennedy was granted a visa. It is reprinted here:

"I came here because of my deep interest and affection for a land settled by the Dutch in the mid-seventeenth century, then taken over by the British, and at last independent; a land in which the native inhabitants were at first subdued, but relations with whom remain a problem to this day; a land which defined itself on a hostile frontier; a land which has tamed rich natural resources through the energetic application of modern technology; a land which once imported slaves, and now must struggle to wipe out the last traces of that former bondage. I refer, of course, to the United States of America.

For two centuries, my own country has struggled to overcome the self-imposed handicap of prejudice and discrimination based on nationality, social class, or race-discrimination profoundly repugnant to the theory and command of our Constitution. Even as my father grew up in Boston, signs told him that 'No Irish Need Apply.' Two generations later President Kennedy became the first

Catholic to head the nation; but how many men of ability had, before 1961, been denied the opportunity to contribute to the nation's progress because they were Catholic, or of Irish extraction? How many sons of Italian or Jewish or Polish parents slumbered in slums-untaught, unlearned, their potential lost forever to the nation and human race? Even today, what price will we pay before we have assured full opportunity to millions of Negro Americans?

Robert and Ethel Kennedy shake hands in Cape Town, South Africa.

In the last five years we have done more to assure equality to our Negro citizens, and to help the deprived, both white and black, than in the hundred years before. But much more remains to be done.

For there are millions of Negroes untrained for the simplest of jobs, and thousands every day denied their full equal rights under the law; and the violence of the disinherited, the insulted and injured, looms over the streets of Harlem and Watts and South Side Chicago.

But a Negro American trains as an astronaut, one of mankind's first explorers into outer space; another is the chief barrister of the United States government, and dozens sit on the benches of court; and another, Dr. Martin Luther King is the second man of African descent to win the Nobel Peace Prize for his nonviolent efforts for social justice between races. We have passed laws prohibiting discrimination in education, in employment, in housing, but these laws alone cannot overcome the heritage of centuries of broken families and stunted children, and poverty and degradation and pain.

So, the road toward equality of freedom is not easy, and great cost and danger march alongside us. We are committed to peaceful and nonviolent change, and that is important for all to understand though all change is unsettling. Still, even in the turbulence of protest and struggle is greater hope for the future, as men learn to claim and achieve for themselves the rights formerly petitioned from others.

And most important of all, all the panoply of government power has been committed to the goal of equality before the law, as we are now committing ourselves to the achievement of equal opportunity in fact.

We must recognize the full human equality of all of our people before God, before the law, and in the councils of government. We must do this, not because it is economically advantageous, although it is not because the laws of God command it, although they do; not because people in other lands wish it so. We must do it for the single and fundamental reason that it is the right thing to do.

We recognize that there are problems and obstacles before the fulfillment of these ideals in the United States, as we recognize that other nations, in Latin America and Asia and Africa, have their own political, economic, and social problems, their unique barriers to the elimination of injustices.

In some, there is concern that change will submerge the rights of a minority, particularly where the minority is of a different race from the majority. We in the United States believe in the protection of minorities; we recognize the contributions they can make and the leadership they can provide; and we do not believe that any people—whether minority, majority, or individual human beings are 'expendable' in the cause of theory or policy. We recognize also that justice between men and nations is imperfect, and that humanity sometimes progresses slowly.

All do not develop in the same manner, or at the same pace. Nations, like men, often march to the beat of different drummers, and the precise solutions of the United States can neither be dictated nor transplanted to others. What is important is that all nations must march toward increasing freedom; toward justice for all; toward a society strong and flexible enough to meet the demands of all its own people, and a world of immense and dizzying change.

In a few hours, the plane that brought me to this country crossed over oceans and countries which have been a crucible of human history. In minutes we traced the migration of men over thousands of years; seconds, the briefest glimpse, and we passed battlefields on which millions of men once struggled and died. We could see no national boundaries, no vast gulfs or high walls dividing people from people; only nature and the works of man—homes and factories and farms everywhere reflecting man's common effort to enrich his life.

Everywhere new technology and communications bring men and nations closer together, the concerns of one inevitably becoming the concerns of all. And our new closeness is stripping away the false masks, the illusion of difference which is at the root of injustice and hate and war. Only earthbound man still clings to the dark and poisoning superstition that his world is bounded by the nearest hill, his universe ended at river shore, his common humanity enclosed in the tight circle of those who share his town and views and the color of his skin. It is your job, the task of the young people of this world, to strip the last remnants of that ancient, cruel belief from the civilization of man.

Each nation has different obstacles and different goals, shaped by the vagaries of history and of experience. Yet as I talk to young people around the world, I am impressed not by the diversity but by the closeness of their goals, their desires and their concerns and their hope for the future. There is discrimination in New York, the racial inequality of apartheid in South Africa, and serfdom in the mountains of Peru. People starve in the streets of India, a former Prime Minister is summarily executed in the Congo, intellectuals go to jail in Russia, and thousands are slaughtered in Indonesia; wealth is lavished on armaments everywhere in the world. These are differing evils; but they are the common works of man. They reflect the imperfections of human justice, the inadequacy of human compassion, the defectiveness of our sensibility toward the sufferings of our fellows; they mark the limit of our ability to use knowledge for the well-being of our fellow human beings throughout the world. And therefore, they call upon common qualities of conscience and indignation, a shared determination to wipe away the unnecessary sufferings of our fellow human beings at home and around the world.

It is these qualities which make our youth today the only true international community. More than this I think that we could agree on what kind of a world we would all want to build. It would be a world of independent nations, moving toward international community, each of which protected and respected the basic human freedoms. It would be a world which demanded of each government that it accept its responsibility to ensure social justice. It would be a world of constantly accelerating economic progress—not material welfare as an end in itself, but as a means to liberate the capacity of every human being to pursue his talents and to pursue his hopes. It would, in short, be a world that we would be proud to have built.

Just to the north of here are lands of challenge and opportunity—rich in natural resources, land and minerals and people. Yet they are also lands confronted by the greatest odds—overwhelming ignorance, internal tensions and strife, and great obstacles of climate and geography. Many of these nations, as colonies, were oppressed and exploited. Yet they have not estranged themselves from the broad traditions of the West; they are hoping and gambling their progress and stability on the chance that we will meet our responsibilities to help them overcome their poverty.

In the world we would like to build, South Africa could play an outstanding role in that effort. This is without question a preeminent repository of the wealth and knowledge and skill of the continent. Here are the greater part of Africa's research scientists and steel production, most of its reservoirs of coal and electric power. Many South Africans have made major contributions to African technical development and world science; the names of some are known wherever men seek to eliminate the ravages of tropical diseases and pestilence. In your faculties and councils, here in this very audience, are hundreds of thousands of men who could transform the lives of millions for all time to come.

But the help and the leadership of South Africa or the United States cannot be accepted if we—within our own countries or in our relations with others—deny individual integrity, human dignity, and the common humanity of man. If we would lead outside our borders, if we would help those who need our assistance, if we would meet our responsibilities to mankind, we must first, all of us, demolish the borders which history has erected between men within our own nations—barriers of race and religion, social class, and ignorance.

Each time a man stands up for an ideal, or acts to improve the lot of others, or strikes out against injustice, he sends forth a tiny ripple of hope, and crossing each other from a million different centers of energy and daring those ripples build a current which can sweep down the mightiest walls of oppression and resistance. (c)

Although 1968 is remembered as a year of violence and death, it was also filled with hope. The vision that Martin Luther King had set in motion during a caravan to the nation's capital continued even after King was killed. It was filled with hope by thousands of volunteers who went door-to-door to elect a Presidential candidate who many believed understood the pain of racism, violence, injustice, and death, having witnessed it politically and experienced it personally. RFK said, "we cannot separate ourselves, no matter where we live from the problems and the troubles and the difficulties that face the whole of the United States."

In Indianapolis, Indiana on April 4, 1968 while campaigning for President, Robert Kennedy delivered a speech to the crowd that had enthusiastically come to support him. His message had drastically changed from his original speech about an exit strategy in the Vietnam War. Bobby had to inform the crowd that

RFK speech in Indianapolis announcing Martin Luther King's death.

Dr. Martin Luther King Jr. had just been shot and killed in Memphis Tennessee. He said,

"We can move in that direction as a country, in greater polarization—black people amongst blacks, and white amongst whites, filled with hatred toward one another. Or we can make an effort, as Martin Luther King did, to understand and to comprehend, and replace that violence, that stain of bloodshed that has spread across our land, with an effort to understand, with compassion and love. What we need in the United States is not division; what we need in the United States is not hatred; what we need in the United States is not violence and

lawlessness, but is love and wisdom, and compassion toward one another, and a feeling of justice toward those who still suffer within our country, whether they be white, or whether they be black."

Riots occurred in major cities across the United States after the assassination of Martin Luther King Jr. No riots occurred in Indianapolis, Indiana.

As he began to move forward to seek the Democratic Party's nomination for the Presidency, it was clear that RFK was carrying on his Brother's penultimate goal of establishing peace, not only in the United States, but worldwide. Like his Brother before him, that endeavor would ultimately cost him his life. There is no money to be made in peace, only war.

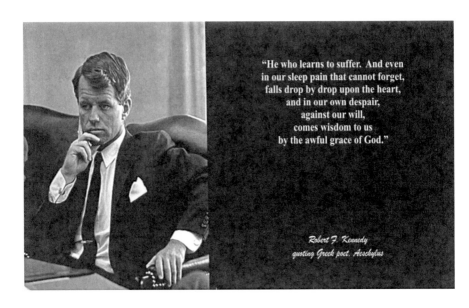

"He who learns to suffer. And even
in our sleep pain that cannot forget,
falls drop by drop upon the heart,
and in our own despair,
against our will,
comes wisdom to us
by the awful grace of God."

Robert F. Kennedy
quoting Greek poet, Aeschylus

Four

<u>The Road to California</u>

Robert Kennedy had been discussing the critical issues of the nation the entire time he served as Senator from New York. Many in the media were assuming he would run against Lyndon Johnson in 1968. Eugene McCarthy announced his intention to run against LBJ on November 30, 1967 based on an anti-Vietnam platform. Robert expressed his concerns with George McGovern (Dem., South Dakota) saying, "I'm worried that you and other people are planning to make early commitments to McCarthy." McGovern assured the Senator he hadn't decided to support any candidate as of yet. In early February 1968, after the Tet Offensive in Vietnam, RFK received a letter from writer Pete Hamill. Hamill's letter said in brief,

"I had been wanting to write you a long letter explaining my reasons why I thought you should make a run for the Presidency this year (1968), but that's too late. I read in the Irish Times this morning that you made a hard announcement, and that small hope is gone along with others that have vanished in the last four years. I suspect that all nations have their historical moment, some moment when it all seems to have been put together as an idea. Our moment was 1960-1963. I don't think it's nostalgia working, or romanticism, I think most Americans feel that way now. The moment is gone now, and we have grown accustomed to living in a country when nobody would protest very much if Jack

Valenti replaced John Gardner. I wanted to say that the fight you might make, would be the fight of honor. I wanted to say that you should run because if you won, the country might be saved. If we have LBJ for another four years, there won't be much of a country left. I've heard the argument that the practical politics which are involved will destroy the Democratic party, you will destroy yourself. I say if you don't run you might destroy the Democratic party, we will end up nationally the way it has in New York. A party filled with decrepit old Bastards like Abe Beam and Rap Brown and young hustlers with blue hair trying to get their bad hands-on highway contracts. It will be a party that says to millions and millions of people that they don't count, that the decisions of 2000 hack polls does. They will say that idealism is a cynical joke. Hard-headed pragmatism is the rule and even if the pragmatist rule in the style of Bonnie and Clyde. I wanted to remind you that in Watts (California) I didn't see pictures of Malcolm X on the walls, I saw pictures of JFK. That is your Capitol in the most cynical sense. It is your obligation of staying true to whatever it was that put those pictures on those walls. I don't think we can afford five summers of blood. I do know this, if a 15-year-old kid is given a choice between Rap Brown and RFK, he might choose the way of sanity. It's only a possibility, but at least there is that choice. I'd give that same kid the choice between Rap Brown and LBJ, and he will probably reach for his revolver. Again, forgive the tone of this letter Bob, but it's not about five cent cigars and chickens in every pot, it's about the country. I don't want to sound like someone telling someone that he should mount the white horse, or that he should destroy his career. I also realize that if you have decided to run, you would face some filthy politics and that there are plenty of people in the country who resent or dislike you. With all of that, I still think the move would have been worth making and I'm sorry you've decided not to make it."

Author Pete Hamill

"RFK carried this letter with him for the next couple of weeks, still deciding on whether to run or not," said press secretary Frank Mankiewicz. "He constantly re-read the letter and focused on JFK's image on the walls of homes in ghetto neighborhoods and realized that his brother's legacy could be continued." This letter influenced Bobby along with the Kerner Commission report on the racial unrest that had affected American cities during the previous summer. The Kerner Commission blamed 'white racism' for the violence, but its findings were largely dismissed by the Johnson administration. RFK asked his advisor, Arthur M. Schlesinger Jr., "How can we possibly survive five more years of Lyndon Johnson?" This comment can directly be tied to the Hamill letter asking if the country can survive five more summers of blood. Bobby's wife, Ethel supported the idea, but initially his younger brother Ted Kennedy did not. Once Bobby made the decision to run, Teddy changed his opinion and completely supported his brother.

RFK speaking in D.C. June 1963.

Bobby's decision to run was finally made when he traveled to California to meet with civil rights activist Cesar Chavez. Kennedy told his aide, Peter Edelman, that he had decided to run but had to figure out how to get McCarthy out of the election. RFK agreed to delay the announcement until after the New Hampshire primary. He was hoping that McCarthy would not have a chance against LBJ in this opening primary. He would be wrong. McCarthy carried 42% of the vote to the incumbent President's 58%. Kennedy knew it was unlikely that the Minnesota Senator would agree to withdraw from the race and decided to formally announce his candidacy.

Washington, D.C. March 16, 1968

"I am today announcing my candidacy for the presidency of the United States.

I do not run for the presidency merely to oppose any man but to propose new policies. I run because I am convinced that this country is on a perilous course and because I have such strong feelings about what must be done, and I feel that I'm obliged to do all that I can.

I run to seek new policies—policies to end the bloodshed in Vietnam and in our cities, policies to close the gaps that now exist between black and white, between rich and poor, between young and old, in this country and around the rest of the world.

I run for the presidency because I want the Democratic Party and the United States of America to stand for hope instead of despair, for reconciliation of men instead of the growing risk of world war.

I run because it is now unmistakably clear that we can change these disastrous, divisive policies only by changing the men who are now making them. For the reality of recent events in Vietnam has been glossed over with illusions.

The Report of the Riot Commission has been largely ignored.

The crisis in gold, the crisis in our cities, the crisis in our farms and in our ghettos have all been met with too little and too late.

No one knows what I know about the extraordinary demands of the presidency can be certain that any mortal can adequately fill that position.

But my service in the National Security Council during the Cuban Missile Crisis, the Berlin crisis of 1961 and 1962, and later the negotiations on Laos and on the Nuclear Test Ban Treaty have taught me something about both the uses and limitations of military power, about the opportunities and the dangers which await our nation in many corners of the globe in which I have traveled.

As a member of the cabinet and member of the Senate I have seen the inexcusable and ugly deprivation which causes children to starve in Mississippi, black citizens to riot in Watts; young Indians to commit suicide on their reservations because they've lacked all hope and they feel they have no future, and proud and able-bodied families to wait out their lives in empty idleness in eastern Kentucky.

I have traveled and I have listened to the young people of our nation and felt their anger about the war that they are sent to fight and about the world they are about to inherit.

In private talks and in public, I have tried in vain to alter our course in Vietnam before it further saps our spirit and our manpower, further raises the risks of wider war, and further destroys the country and the people it was meant to save.

I cannot stand aside from the contest that will decide our nation's future and our children's future.

The remarkable New Hampshire campaign of Senator Eugene McCarthy has proven how deep are the present divisions within our party and within our country. Until that was publicly clear, my presence in the race would have been seen as a clash of personalities rather than issues.

But now that the fight is on and over policies which I have long been challenging, I must enter the race. The fight is just beginning, and I believe that I can win.

Finally, my decision reflects no personal animosity or disrespect toward President Johnson. He served President Kennedy with the utmost loyalty and was extremely kind to me and members of my family in the difficult months which followed the events of November of 1963.

I have often commended his efforts in health, in education, and in many other areas, and I have the deepest sympathy for the burden that he carries today.

But the issue is not personal. It is our profound differences over where we are heading and what we want to accomplish.

I do not lightly dismiss the dangers and the difficulties of challenging an incumbent President. But

these are not ordinary times, and this is not an ordinary election.

At stake is not simply the leadership of our party and even our country. It is our right to moral leadership of this planet."

With the formal announcement that RFK was in the 1968 Presidential race, all eyes were now focused on the next primary, April 2nd, Wisconsin. President Johnson was facing two anti-war challengers, both sitting members of the U.S. Senate and both extremely popular with the younger generation. Early polling in Wisconsin showed McCarthy beating Johnson badly. McCarthy was polling near 70%, LBJ was only at 12%. Facing declining health and low political forecasts in upcoming primaries, Johnson did the unthinkable.

On March 31, 1968, at the end of a televised address on Vietnam, Johnson shocked the nation by announcing that, "he would not seek, and he would not accept another term as your President." Johnson used the rest of his term to support his Vice President, Hubert H. Humphrey. LBJ was secretly supporting his Vice President although publicly he remained neutral on the topic. Johnson was hoping that he could end the conflict in Vietnam before the election in November and therefore boost his Vice President's chances of securing the nomination and Presidency. After LBJ's withdrawal, the Wisconsin primary on April 2nd was won by McCarthy 56% to Humphrey's 35%. Kennedy only received 6% of the vote. The Pennsylvania primary on April 23 was also a rout for McCarthy who took 71% of the vote. Humphrey was unaware of LBJ's announcement and was not on many of the ballots but immediately announced his formal candidacy on April 27, 1968.

LBJ televised speech on the Vietnam War on March 31, 1968. At the end of this speech, he announced he would not seek the Presidency in 1968.

Prior to the announcement from Johnson, Bobby had already announced his intention to run against McCarthy in the Indiana primary on March 27, 1968. Bobby realized that the only way to attract more support was to face McCarthy face to face. After all, in 1967, it was McCarthy who first voiced displeasure with the Vietnam War. Bobby had been Attorney General under his brother's and Johnson's administration. While JFK sought to pull out of the Vietnam War with NSAM 263, LBJ immediately changed course and increased the U.S. military presence in Vietnam with NSAM 273. The following images of NSAM 273 were presented to Johnson, not JFK, on November 21, 1963. They are declassified from the LBJ Library.

THE WHITE HOUSE

WASHINGTON

- EYES ONLY   October 11, 1963

NATIONAL SECURITY ACTION MEMORANDUM NO. 263

TO: Secretary of State
           Secretary of Defense
           Chairman of the Joint Chiefs of Staff

SUBJECT: South Vietnam

At a meeting on October 5, 1963, the President considered the
recommendations contained in the report of Secretary McNamara
and General Taylor on their mission to South Vietnam.

The President approved the military recommendations contained
in Section I B (1-3) of the report, but directed that no formal
announcement be made of the implementation of plans to withdraw 1,000 U.S. miltitary personnel by the end of 1963.

After discussion of the remaining recommendations of the report,
the President approved an instruction to Ambassador Lodge which
is set forth in State Department telegram No. 534 to Saigon.

McGeorge Bundy

Copy furnished:
   Director of Central Intelligence
   Administrator, Agency for International Development

                                              cc:
                                                 Mr. Bundy
                                                 Mr. Forrestal
                                                 Mr. Johnson
              TOP SECRET - EYES ONLY NSC Files

DECLASSIFIED
E. O. 11652, SEC. 3(E), 5(D), 5(E) A+D 11

Committee Print of Pentagon Papers
BY HSZ   NARS, DATE 7/15/77

NSAM 263 dated October 11, 1963.

11/21/63
DRAFT

TOP SECRET

NATIONAL SECURITY ACTION MEMORANDUM NO. _____

The President has reviewed the discussions of South Vietnam which occurred in Honolulu, and has discussed the matter further with Ambassador Lodge. He directs that the following guidance be issued to all concerned:

1. It remains the central object of the United States in South Vietnam to assist the people and Government of that country to win their contest against the externally directed and supported Communist conspiracy. The test of all decisions and (U. S.) actions in this area should be the effectiveness of their contribution to this purpose.

2. The objectives of the United States with respect to the withdrawal of U. S. military personnel remain as stated in the White House statement of October 2, 1963.

3. It is a major interest of the United States Government that the present provisional government of South Vietnam should be assisted in consolidating itself and in holding and developing increased public support. All U. S. officers should conduct themselves with this objective in view.

4. It is of the highest importance that the United States Government avoid either the appearance or the reality of public recrimination from one part of it against another, and the President expects that all senior officers of the Government will take energetic steps to insure that they and their

TOP SECRET

NSAM 273 original draft. (Notice date in upper left corner, Nov. 21, 1963).

NSAM 273 completely reversed JFK's course in Vietnam. Ironically, this draft was presented to LBJ and approved on November 21, 1963! Why was the Military Industrial Complex writing policy on the Vietnam War and giving the initial draft to the current Vice President instead of JFK on November 21, 1963? This information wasn't released until many years after Robert Kennedy's death. Notice this copy is on file at the LBJ Library.

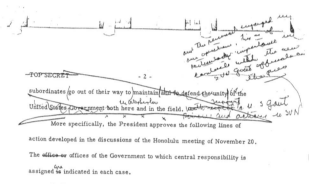

TOP SECRET   - 2 -

subordinates go out of their way to maintain and to defend the unity of the
United States Government both here and in the field.

More specifically, the President approves the following lines of

action developed in the discussions of the Honolulu meeting of November 20.

The office or offices of the Government to which central responsibility is

assigned is indicated in each case.

    5. We should concentrate our own efforts, and insofar as possible

we should persuade the Government of South Vietnam to concentrate its

efforts, on the critical situation in the Mekong Delta. This concentration

should include not only military but political, economic, social, educational

and informational effort. We should seek to turn the tide not only of battle

but of belief, and we should seek to increase not only our control of land but

the productivity of this area, wherever the proceeds can be held for the

advantage of anti-Communist forces.

(Action: The whole country team under the direct supervision of the

Ambassador.)

    6. Programs of military and economic assistance should be

maintained at such levels that their magnitude and effectiveness in the eyes

of the Vietnamese Government do not fall below the levels sustained by the

United States in the time of the Diem Government. This does not exclude

arrangements for economy on the MAP account with respect to accounting

for ammunition and any other readjustments which are possible as between

                        TOP SECRET

NSAM 273, page 2.

MAP and other U. S. defense resources. Special attention should be given

to the expansion of the import, distribution, and effective use of fertilizer

for the Delta.

(Action: AID and DOD as appropriate.)

7. With respect to action against North Vietnam, there should

be a detailed plan for the development of additional Government of Vietnam

resources, especially for sea-going activity, and such planning should

indicate the time and investment necessary to achieve a wholly new level *and higher*

of effectiveness in this field of action.

(Action: *State,* DOD, and CIA)

8. With respect to Laos, a plan should be developed for military *and submitted for approval by higher authority*

operations up to a line up to 50 kilometers inside Laos, together with

political plans for minimizing the international hazards of such an enter-

prise. Since it is agreed that operational responsibility for such undertakings

should pass from CAS to MACV, this plan should provide an alternative *include*

a redefined method of political liaison for such operations, since their timing and *control over*

include for character can have an intimate relation to the fluctuating situation in Laos.

(Action: State, DOD and CIA.)

9. It was agreed in Honolulu that the situation in Cambodia is of the

first importance for South Vietnam, and it is therefore urgent that we should

lose no opportunity to exercise a favorable influence upon that country. In

particular, measures should be undertaken to satisfy ourselves completely

NSAM 273, Page 3 (note this is from LBJ Library).

that recent charges from Cambodia are groundless, and we should put / 9)
ourselves in a position to offer to the Cambodians a full opportunity to
satisfy themselves on this same point.

(Action: State)

   10. In connection with paragraphs 7 and 8 above, it is desired
that we should develop as strong and persuasive a case as possible to
demonstrate to the world the degree to which the Viet Cong is controlled,
sustained and supplied from Hanoi, through Laos and other channels. In
short, we need a more contemporary version of the Jorden Report, as
powerful and complete as possible.

(Action: Department of State with other agencies as necessary.)

                                        McGeorge Bundy

NSAM 273, Page 4

Despite his aides advising him not to run against Senator McCarthy in Indiana, Bobby filed the forms to run in the Indiana primary on March 28, 1968. At the Indiana Statehouse, Kennedy told a cheering crowd that Indiana was important to his campaign. He said, "If we can win in Indiana, we can win in every other state, and win when we go to the convention in August."

Bobby traveled to Indiana the following week with planned stops in South Bend, Elkhart, Muncie, and Indianapolis. He appeared at the West Side Democratic & Civic Club near the University of Notre Dame campus on April 4, 1968. It was vital for him to capture the college vote and more importantly, the Polish vote in northern Indiana. Could he defeat another anti-war candidate in Senator McCarthy? Could he win in a three-horse race with Indiana Governor, Roger Branigin, a stand-in for Hubert Humphrey and endorsed by the Indianapolis Star?

After stumping in South Bend, RFK traveled to Muncie Indiana to speak at Ball State University. He said, "the 1968 election would determine the direction that the United States is going to move towards and to examine everything. Do not take anything for granted." He continued to speak about his concerns about poverty and hunger, lawlessness and violence, the economy, not only in Indiana, but the entire United States. He finished his speech by saying, "Americans must have a moral obligation and to make an honest effort to understand one another and move forward together." From Muncie, he took a short flight to Indianapolis. Before leaving Muncie, Bobby was notified that Dr. King had been shot in Memphis but did not have an updated condition. Like his brother five years prior, RFK was consumed with grief. When he arrived in Indianapolis, he was notified that Dr. Martin Luther King, Jr. had succumbed to his wounds. It was Bobby's duty to inform the cheerful crowd of the horrific news from Memphis.

When he took the stage at Seventeenth and Broadway, the crowd was enthusiastic. Bobby can be heard in film clips saying, "Do they (audience) know what has happened?" Unlike today where news stories travel around the world in minutes, the local Indiana news outlets had not received word of Martin Luther King's assassination. Robert addressed the crowd.

"I have bad news for you, for all of our fellow citizens, and people who love peace all over the world, and that is that Martin Luther King was shot and killed tonight.

Martin Luther King dedicated his life to love and to justice for his fellow human beings, and he died because of that effort.

In this difficult day, in this difficult time for the United States, it is perhaps well to ask what kind of a nation we are and what direction we want to move in. For those of you who are black—considering the evidence there evidently is that there were white people who were responsible—you can be filled with bitterness, with hatred, and a desire for revenge. We can move in that direction as a country, in great polarization—black people amongst black, white people amongst white, filled with hatred toward one another.

Or we can make an effort, as Martin Luther King did, to understand and to comprehend, and to replace that

violence, that stain of bloodshed that has spread across our land, with an effort to understand with compassion and love.

For those of you who are black and are tempted to be filled with hatred and distrust at the injustice of such an act, against all white people, I can only say that I feel in my own heart the same kind of feeling. I had a member of my family killed, but he was killed by a white man. But we have to make an effort in the United States, we have to make an effort to understand, to go beyond these rather difficult times.

My favorite poet was Aeschylus. He wrote: "In our sleep, pain which cannot forget falls drop by drop upon the heart until, in our own despair, against our will, comes wisdom through the awful grace of God."

What we need in the United States is not division; what we need in the United States is not hatred; what we need in the United States is not violence or lawlessness; but love and wisdom, and compassion toward one another, and a feeling of justice toward those who still suffer within our country, whether they be white or they be black.

So, I shall ask you tonight to return home, to say a prayer for the family of Martin Luther King, that's true, but more importantly to say a prayer for our own country, which all of us love—a prayer for understanding and that compassion of which I spoke.

We can do well in this country. We will have difficult times; we've had difficult times in the past; we will have difficult times in the future. It is not the end of violence; it is not the end of lawlessness; it is not the end of disorder.

But the vast majority of white people and the vast majority of black people in this country want to live together, want to improve the quality of our life, and want justice for all human beings who abide in our land.

Let us dedicate ourselves to what the Greeks wrote so many years ago: to tame the savageness of man and make gentle the life of this world.

Let us dedicate ourselves to that and say a prayer for our country and for our people."

The casket containing Martin Luther King on his final trip home to Atlanta.

Robert Kennedy worked behind the scenes after making his late-night speech about Dr. King's assassination. He had arranged for an American Airlines Electra jet for Coretta Scott King to take off from Atlanta at 9:15 a.m., the morning of April 5. It was to arrive in Memphis approximately 70 minutes later. Coretta never left the aircraft. She simply cried on the shoulder of a companion as her husband's casket was loaded onto the plane for the final journey home to Atlanta. An unidentified SCLC official in Atlanta was asked who Dr. Martin Luther King's pallbearers would be. "Every black man in this country," he responded.

Coretta King with family and friends at Spelman College service.

Robert Kennedy remained in Indiana and continued to refine his message to conservative Indiana voters. On April 9th he joined Jackie Kennedy in Atlanta for Dr. King's funeral. King's death gave Kennedy the purpose his candidacy had lost with Lyndon Johnson's withdrawal. His vision became a broadened version of King's own fight for the disenfranchised. "Martin

Luther King Jr. represented the best in our nation," RFK said, "Dr. King lived and died not only for the Negro but for all Americans—and, in particular, for the youth of our nation." Kennedy maligned the FBI by telling Pete Hamill, "It's very interesting that they can't find the killer of Martin Luther King, but they can track down some 22-year-old who might have burned his draft card."

After Dr. King's death more than 100 U.S. cities erupted in arson and violence. Primarily because of Robert Kennedy's speech, Indianapolis remained calm, as did Martin Luther King's hometown of Atlanta. Dr. King's funeral rites were observed in a private service at Ebenezer Baptist Church, where King had been co-pastor with his father. Sadly, MLK's mother, Alberta (69) was shot and killed while playing the organ at Ebenezer Baptist Church on June 30, 1974. The killer, Marcus Wayne Chenault Jr., also killed 69-year-old church deacon, Edward Boykin.

In the days before the commemoration, King's body laid in state at Spelman College. Over 1,300 mourners were inside Ebenezer's walls for the service, an estimated 50,000 were listening outside over loudspeakers, and millions of people watched the service over television. After the private service, King's casket was carried through the crowd to a waiting mule-drawn wagon and led through the city's streets to Morehouse College, where a public commemoration was held. More than 100,000 people joined the solemn procession through the streets of Atlanta. Civil rights leaders, politicians, celebrities from all arts, entertainment, and sports as well as public servants and friends all followed Dr. Martin Luther King one last time.

Dr. Martin Luther King's casket driven through the streets of Atlanta with over 100,000 dignitaries following.

After Dr. King's funeral, Bobby immediately returned to Indiana on April 10th to concentrate on the upcoming May 7th Indiana primary. Leading up to the primary, RFK delivered a speech before the Indianapolis real estate board on May 2, 1968. In the days immediately before the primary, Kennedy and McCarthy both had issues with Governor Roger Branigin.

Branigan was a stand-in for LBJ/Humphrey since LBJ had decided not to run and Hubert couldn't get on the ballots in time. Branigan campaigned in nearly all of Indiana's 92 counties, while McCarthy's strategy was to concentrate on rural areas and small towns. Bobby visited central and southern Indiana on April 22 and 23, including a whistle-stop railroad tour aboard the Wabash Cannonball. The primary was held May 7th. Kennedy won with 42% of the vote, Branigan was second with 31% and McCarthy only garnered 27%, a devastating blow to his campaign. With the victory in Indiana, RFK looked next to Nebraska.

RFK on campaign trail.

Using the momentum from Indiana, RFK frequented Nebraska several times. McCarthy assumed he was in complete control in Nebraska and stopped to campaign there just once, an egregious mistake Hillary Clinton repeated in 2016 by ignoring states she felt confident she would win. The ensuing RFK victory in Nebraska was significant by demonstrating he could reach rural voters with issues concerning and agriculture. Bobby won the primary on May 14th with 51.4% of the vote to McCarthy's 31%.

Bobby declared that with McCarthy and himself garnering over 80% of the vote, this was "a smashing repudiation" of the Johnson-Humphrey administration. Momentum was swinging towards Kennedy with Oregon on the horizon.

Oregon, however, posed a larger problem for Kennedy's campaign. RFK had been running in most states on a platform of poverty, hunger and minority issues which did not resonate with Oregon voters. For the first time, RFK went on the attack of Senator McCarthy, criticizing his repeal of the poll tax in the Voting Rights Act of 1965 and his voting against a minimum wage law. McCarthy responded with charges that while Attorney General, Kennedy illegally taped Martin Luther King Jr. Bobby could not dispute his record, even though he personally was against the wiretaps that were demanded by J. Edgar Hoover.

RFK, two sons, and family friend John Glenn at Disneyland the day before his assassination.

Kennedy responded with a gambling term referred to as, 'all-in.' He said, "I think that if I get beaten in any primary, I am not a very viable candidate." In response to this comment, Bobby campaigned sixteen hours a day in the weeks before the election, sending a clear message to California, South Dakota, and New Jersey that he was the candidate to defeat. Bobby, just like his brother before him, realized that an attractive wife is essentially an 'Ace in the Hole' card. His wife Ethel and family friend, astronaut John Glenn began campaigning for him in Portland. McCarthy was already there campaigning. Mankiewicz claimed that McCarthy and Humphrey were banding together against Kennedy.

On May 28th, McCarthy won the Oregon primary with 44.7% of the vote to Kennedy's 38.8%. This was a devastating blow to Bobby and his campaign, having previously commented, "if I get beaten in a primary, I'm not a very viable candidate." Primaries in California, New Jersey and South Dakota lie ahead. Humphrey had been raised as a child in South Dakota a neighboring state to McCarthy. South Dakota became ground zero. Kennedy had to win both California and South Dakota if his campaign was to continue until the Democratic National Convention.

Senator McCarthy's campaign in California was organized and well-funded. McCarthy, just like Hillary Clinton in 2016, relied upon his close connections and used what money was appropriated for South Dakota for the California campaign. Bobby Kennedy was relying on his voter appeal and college voting in California. Bobby knew he was the weakest candidate in South Dakota given the family ties of McCarthy and Humphrey. As JFK had done before him, RFK used television to strengthen his position.

McCarthy (having microphone placed) during roundtable debate with RFK.

On June 1, during the final days of the campaign, Kennedy and McCarthy met for a televised debate. Kennedy, unbeknownst to McCarthy, had paid for the debate in California to be broadcast on most major television networks in South Dakota. Two pivotal events occurred after the debate. One, Kennedy picked up undecided voters 2-1 against McCarthy. Two, the voters in South Dakota, just like JFK before him, were infatuated with Bobby's charisma, honesty, and appearance. Two days later, RFK made a whirlwind trip through California with stops in San Diego, San Francisco, Long Beach, and Los Angeles. He won the South Dakota primary 50% to 20%. He won in California by 46% to McCarthy's 42%. On June 4th, RFK had McCarthy on the ropes with his victories in both states. Early in the morning of June 5th,

Bobby decided to deliver an acceptance speech. These would become the last public words ever spoken by Robert F. Kennedy.

Robert & Ethel Kennedy after winning the California primary, June 4, 1968.

"Every time we turn
our heads the other way,
when we see the law flouted,
when we tolerate what we know to be wrong,
when we close our eyes
and ears to the corrupt because
we are too busy or too frightened,
when we fail to speak up and speak out,
we strike a blow against
freedom and decency and justice."

Robert F. Kennedy

Five

The Ambassador Hotel

The unimaginable happened. Not that Robert F. Kennedy won the California Democratic Primary, but that once again, promises of peace were obliterated by a cascade of carefully calculated bullets intent on shattering the American dream.

After winning the primary late in the evening of June 4, 1968, Robert Kennedy addressed his supporters in the Embassy Room of the Ambassador hotel shortly after midnight. These were his final public remarks:

RFK's final remarks, Embassy Room, Ambassador Hotel June 5, 1968.

"What I think is quite clear is that we can work together in the last analysis and that what has been going on in the United States over the last three years, the divisions, the violence, the disenchantment with our society, the divisions whether it's between blacks and whites, between the poor and the more affluent, or between age groups or on the war in Vietnam, that we can start to work together," Kennedy said.

"We are a great country, an unselfish country, a compassionate country. And I intend to make that my basis for running," he said. "So, my thanks to all of you, and now it's on to Chicago and let's win there."

Robert and Ethel Kennedy greet supporters at the Ambassador Hotel.

Immediately after this short speech, RFK was escorted away by Karl Uecker, maître d'hôtel through the hotel kitchen. He was protected by former FBI agent William Barry and two former athlete bodyguards, Rafer Johnson and Rosy Grier. Bobby was shaking hands with the hotel staff and was in the process of shaking the hand of 17-year-old busboy Juan Romero when shots rang out.

Robert Kennedy shaking hands moments before being shot.

The official government explanation regarding the assassination of Robert Kennedy is a complete fabrication from start to finish. The LAPD incident report should be considered alongside Mark Twain and Grimm's Fairy Tales as some of the best fictional writing ever. The report states that 24-year-old Jordanian immigrant, Sirhan Bishara Sirhan fired eight shots with his .22 caliber Iver Johnson Cadet revolver. Three shots hit Mr. Kennedy; the other five bullets hit the individuals noted below:

Paul Schrade—United Auto Workers Union and Kennedy's campaign labor chair.
Ira Goldstein—A 19-year-old radio reporter for Continental News Service.
William Weisel—Associate news director for ABC News.
Irwin Stroll—A 17-year-old campaign volunteer.
Elizabeth Evans—A Democratic activist.

What the report fails to mention is the other five shots which were fired into the walls and ceiling of the kitchen pantry. This would mean that 13 shots were fired. Are we to believe that Sirhan Sirhan could empty his revolver, hit six different people with those eight bullets, reload the gun and fire five more shots before Johnson, Grier, FBI agent Barry and writer George

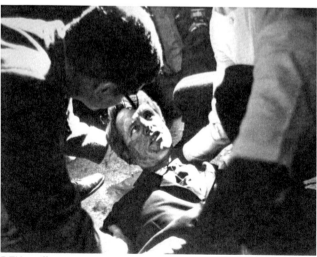

RFK, still conscious, being attended to by Juan Romero.

Plimpton could detain the would-be assassin? As Kennedy lay
seriously wounded, Romero pressed a rosary into his hand. FBI
Agent Barry placed his jacket under Bobby's head. Kennedy
asked, "Is everybody OK?" Romero tried to assure him, "Yes,
everybody's OK." Kennedy turned his head towards Paul
Schrade, lying near him and said, "Everything's going to be OK
Paul."

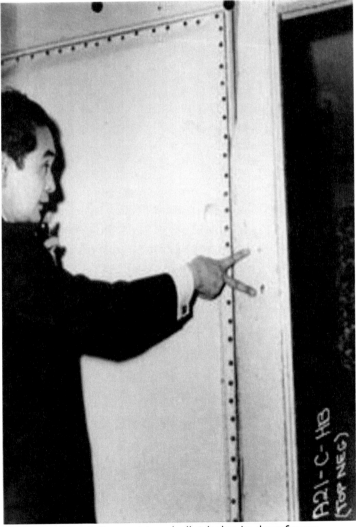

Dr. Noguchi pointing out two bullet holes in door frame.

After being shot, Kennedy remained semiconscious during the approximately 17 minutes he lie dying on the floor. Immediately after the shooting, Stephen E. Smith, RFK's campaign manager, announced over the microphone that a doctor was urgently needed in the hotel kitchen. Five physicians who had been in the ballroom during RFK's victory speech responded. The five physicians included Stanley Abo, a

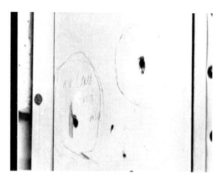

Police notate two more bullet holes, lower in position than Noguchi's bullets

radiologist; Richard O. Dean, an internist and relative of Reverend Martin Luther King Jr.; Ross M. Miller Jr., a trauma surgeon; and George Lambert, a physician with American Airlines. The fifth physician, Marvin Esher, noted that the Senator had shallow breathing with a heart rate of 50–60 beats per minute. Kennedy's left eye was closed; his right eye was open and deviated to the right. He was still able to move all four extremities. Dr. Abo noted that Kennedy was losing consciousness and examined the Senator's head wound. A small blood clot had formed at the site of the bullet hole in the right posterior auricular region, behind Bobby's right ear. Abo assumed that blood was accumulating in Kennedy's head and inserted his finger into the hole to disrupt the clot. With that action, the clot dislodged, blood flowed freely from the bullet hole, and Kennedy's consciousness briefly improved. This description is eerily akin to the initial events surrounding Abraham Lincoln's assassination. After John Wilkes Booth had shot Lincoln,

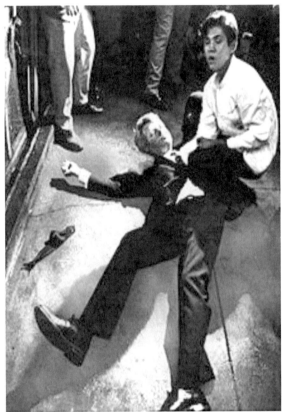

RFK comforted by Juan Romero in kitchen pantry.

Dr. Charles A. Leale was the first physician to treat the President. When Leale examined the President, Lincoln's respiratory rate was very irregular and slow. Dr. Leale inserted his finger into the entrance wound behind Lincoln's left ear, which disrupted a clot, allowing blood to drain and pressure within the skull to decrease. Similar to what was observed with Senator Kennedy, this action resulted in an improvement in Lincoln's respiratory effort, however, it did not change the ultimate outcome for Lincoln any more than it did for Kennedy. (a)

At 12:17 a.m. the switchboard operator at the Ambassador Hotel notified the LAPD that Senator Kennedy had been shot. The LAPD contacted Central Receiving Hospital and requested that an ambulance be dispatched to transport Kennedy. The hospital was two miles away. The ambulance personnel arrived with a stretcher to see Senator Kennedy lying on the floor with blood around his head. Before losing consciousness, Kennedy said, "Don't lift me." These were believed to be his last words.

Ambulance arriving at hospital with Senator Kennedy.

When the Senator arrived at Central Receiving Hospital, he was unconscious with a fixed gaze; he was not breathing, his pulse was hard to detect, and his blood pressure could not be measured. He was immediately attended to by Dr. V. Faustin

Bazilauskas. A cutdown procedure at Kennedy's ankle provided intravenous access. The medical team inserted an oral airway, placed a respirator mask to provide positive pressure ventilation, and then began chest compressions, which continued for the next ten minutes. Kennedy received adrenalin and intravenous boluses of dextran and albumin. His blood pressure returned to (systolic/diastolic) 150/90 and some respiratory effort was observed. Dr. Bazilauskas and another attending surgeon, Dr. Albert Holt, quickly realized that they were not able to offer the care needed for the severity of the head injury. If the medical personnel who picked Kennedy up at the Ambassador had known prior to their arrival that he had a gunshot wound to the head, they probably would have taken him directly to Good Samaritan Hospital for treatment. Dr. Holt knew the neurosurgeons at Good Samaritan Hospital and called the senior surgeon, Dr. Henry Cuneo, to arrange for his transfer there. Since he was uncertain whether the other bullet wounds in Kennedy's right posterior chest had penetrated the thorax, Dr. Holt also called Dr. Bert Meyers, the chief of thoracic surgery at Good Samaritan. Dr. Holt accompanied the Senator in the ambulance so that he could communicate directly with the neurosurgery and thoracic surgery teams.

The distance from Central Receiving Hospital to Good Samaritan Hospital was 0.4 miles, approximately two blocks. Even by 2023 standards, the thirty-minute delay in transferring hospitals probably would not have saved RFK's life. He arrived at the fifth-floor intensive care unit (ICU) at approximately 1:00 a.m. He was initially treated by two surgical residents, Drs. Paul A. Ironside and Hubert Humble. A tracheostomy tube was placed just after his arrival. The Senator was fully disrobed, and the other two injuries were inspected. There was a gunshot wound on the right side of his back. Radiographic findings suggested that the bullet was lodged in the subcutaneous tissue of the neck. This injury was not considered life threatening. In addition, there were wounds in the right armpit and right shoulder, but no corresponding bullets were found on x-ray films. The chest surgeons determined that no bullets had entered the thorax. Kennedy had significant hypertension (systolic pressure 280 mm Hg) when he arrived at the Good Samaritan ICU. Once the tracheostomy had been completed, his blood pressure improved. At the scene of the shooting, Kennedy had displayed diminished motor activity on the left side of his body. By the time he was

Newspaper headlines of Robert Kennedy being shot.

evaluated at Good Samaritan Hospital he had lost all motor activity in response to pain. Whole blood was administered to replace the continued bleeding from the bullet wound in the mastoid region.

Kennedy was transferred to the operating room on the ninth floor of Good Samaritan at 2:45 a.m., 2 hours and 30 minutes after the shooting. The operation began at 3:10 a.m. The senior neurosurgeon was Dr. Henry Cuneo, an associate clinical professor of neurosurgery at the University of Southern California. Other members of the surgical team included Dr. Maxwell Andler of the University of California at Los Angeles Medical School and Dr. Nat Downes Reid of the University of Southern California Medical School.

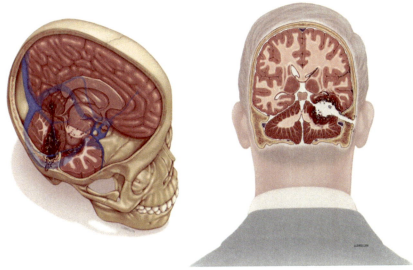

Artist's reconstruction of RFK's head wounds based on autopsy notes.

Preoperative radiographs demonstrated significant bone fragments within the brain functional tissue. As was the standard of the day, the surgeons believed that they needed to remove as many bone and bullet fragments as possible in addition to obtaining control of intracranial bleeding. The operation took over 3 hours and 45 minutes to complete. After the surgeons had created several burr holes near the bullet entrance wound, a 5-cm craniotomy flap was elevated. This resulted in the return of the Senator's spontaneous respiration. During the operation, portions of the occipital lobe and right cerebellum were debrided of devitalized tissue. Bleeding from the petrous sinus was eventually controlled. (The superior petrosal sinus is a part of the dural venous sinus system that drains venous blood and cerebrospinal fluid circulating with the cranial cavity.) Intraoperatively, Kennedy was given dexamethasone and mannitol to help control cerebral edema. At the end of the operation, he was placed on a cooling blanket. He gained some motor activity on the right side of his body, as shown by his response to a pinprick, but there was still a poor response to painful stimulation along his entire left side. (a)

During Kennedy's brief postoperative course, several neurosurgeons from around the country were consulted. Dr. Cuneo called Dr. J. Lawrence Pool to discuss the case. Dr. Pool was chief of neurosurgery at the Neurological Institute of New York. He had completed his medical degree at the University of Pennsylvania and trained in neurosurgery at the Neurological Institute of New York. During his conversation with Dr. Cuneo, Dr. Pool stated that given the damage, even if Kennedy could survive the initial assault, his neurological outcome would be tragic.

Dr. James L. Poppen.

Pierre Salinger, one of the Senator's campaign managers and a friend of the Kennedy family, called Dr. James L. Poppen, a neurosurgeon at Boston's Lahey Clinic, at 4:00 a.m. on June 5, while RFK was still in surgery. Salinger contacted Lyndon Johnson and asked if he could authorize Air Force One to fly to Boston and transport Dr. Poppen to Los Angeles. LBJ denied his request. Salinger asked if Dr. Poppen could fly immediately to Los Angeles and consult on the case. Dr. Poppen, who had attended Rush Medical School in Chicago and joined the Lahey Clinic in 1933, serving as its Chief of Neurosurgery from 1957 to 1964. Poppen had maintained a long relationship with the Kennedys and had treated other members of the family. Vice President Hubert H. Humphrey was contacted by Salinger and arranged for the Air Force (not Air Force One) to transport Dr. Poppen to Los Angeles. Dr. Poppen arrived just before 10:00 a.m. on June 5, approximately three hours after the operation was finished. When Poppen examined Kennedy, he thought the prognosis was grave. He continued to consult with Dr. Cuneo and his team and acted as a liaison to the Kennedy family.

Early in the morning of June 5, family members and friends were hastily making plans for Los Angeles. The voice of reasoning seemed absent. "What madness is afoot?" asked Bob Considine, Hearst newspaper columnist. He continued, "We're sick. The assassin has 200 million heads. One is yours; one is mine." Kennedy adviser and friend, Arthur Schlesinger Jr., said, "We are a violent people with a violent history, and the instinct for violence has seeped into our national life." Rev. Billy Graham said, "I don't weep often, but today, I wept for my country."

In the initial postoperative period, Kennedy was relatively stable. By 6:00 p.m., on June 5, approximately 11 hours after surgery, his condition began to deteriorate. Presumably, Kennedy's intracerebral pressure had started to rise, because his electroencephalogram readings became flat, and he lost his respiratory effort. He never regained consciousness. His heart was beating, but the line on the brain monitor was flat. A neurosurgeon told reporters that given the brain damage caused by one of the bullets, "I fear the outcome may be extremely tragic." Press secretary Mankiewicz told reporters that Kennedy's medical team "is concerned over his continuing failure to show improvement and is extremely critical as to life."

Frank Mankiewicz answering questions outside of Good Samaritan Hospital.

Bobby was clinically brain dead but neither Ethel nor Teddy could make the difficult decision to end Bobby's life. This decision was made by Jacqueline Kennedy. She ordered the respirator shut down and signed the consent form at 1:20 a.m. (b) Robert Francis Kennedy died at 1:44 a.m. Shortly after 2:00 a.m., Frank Mankiewicz read these words:

"Senator Robert Francis Kennedy died at 1:44 a.m., June 6, 1968. With Senator Kennedy at the time of his death were his wife, Ethel; his sisters, Mrs. Stephen Smith, Mrs. Patricia Lawford; and his brother-in-law, Mr. Stephen Smith. He was 42 years old. Thank you."

Although not mentioned in the official Mankiewicz statement, others were present when Robert Kennedy died including Jackie Kennedy, his son Joseph, and William McCormack of St. Patrick's Cathedral in New York. Two of Bobby's other children, Kathleen and Robert Jr., family friend's, Pierre Salinger and Coretta Scott King were also in the hospital at the time of his death.

(L to R) Joan Kennedy, Sargent Shriver and Jackie leaving Good Samaritan.

Coretta Scott King leaving Good Samaritan Hospital after visiting Kennedy.

Unlike his brother, Robert Kennedy received what has been called, 'the perfect autopsy,' because of the attention to detail by LA Coroner, Dr. Thomas Noguchi. Noguchi had been working with the LA Coroner's office since 1961 and had already performed an autopsy involving a celebrity with Marilyn Monroe in 1962. He would become the Coroner of LA County from 1967-1982. He has since been labeled, 'The Coroner of the Stars.'

Dr. Noguchi performed the autopsy immediately on June 6, 1968 and concluded Kennedy had sustained four gunshot injuries. One bullet completely passed through his clothing without hitting any muscle or skeletal tissue. The first bullet entered the back on the right side, lodging at the base of the neck in the subcutaneous space. This 'neck bullet' entered just below bullet #1 entry, near the shoulder blade (scapula). A 'deformed' .22 caliber bullet was recovered at the 6th cervical vertebra

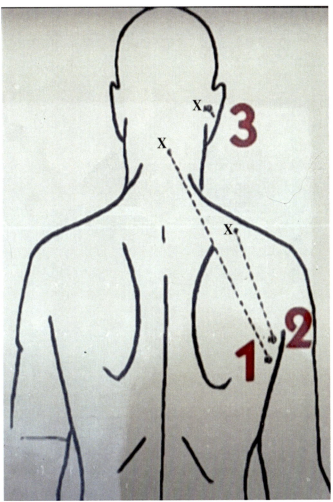

Numbers indicate entrance wounds, 'X' is location of bullet upon autopsy.

(neck/spine). Direction was right to left, back to front and upward.

The second bullet that hit Kennedy entered the right axilla posteriorly and exited near the right clavicle. This wound was a 'through and through' of the right shoulder, with no deflection within the body—it went in a clean line entering from the back and exiting the front. The direction was right to left, back to front and upward. This bullet was never recovered. There were gun powder granules on the dermis. Neither of these injuries caused life-threatening harm.

The fatal shot traveled from right to left, slightly to the front and upwards. There was no exit wound, and it had entered from behind Kennedy's right ear. The fragments that were recovered from this bullet could not be matched to any weapon. The lethal injury to the right posterior auricular region had associated powder burns on the skin, and therefore Noguchi stated that the gun was within three inches when the shooting occurred. Powder residue was found with heat and blast effects visible. Noguchi also stated that the head shot was probably the first to hit Senator Kennedy. Examination of the intracranial contents showed extensive injury to the right cerebellum and right occipital cortex. There were multiple bone and bullet fragments scattered across the brain tissue, and evidence of epidural, subdural, and subarachnoid hemorrhage. There was also evidence of brainstem herniation due to cerebral edema. Damage to the brainstem was likely due to this herniation and not from direct trauma. Both the right middle cerebral artery and the petrous sinus were injured by bullet and bone fragments and were the predominant source of the bleeding. After physical examination of the body, Noguchi evaluated the gun, bullets, Kennedy's clothes, and ballistics tests. The discrepancy between eyewitness reports that Sirhan came no closer than 12 to 18 inches from Kennedy when the shooting occurred, and that he was always in front of Senator Kennedy, and the Noguchi report, which stated that the gun was within 1-3" of the right ear at the time of the shooting, (from behind) was not highlighted in the autopsy report. Noguchi, in his later writings, makes it clear that his report did not imply that Sirhan was the lone shooter, leaving the door open for conspiracy theorists.

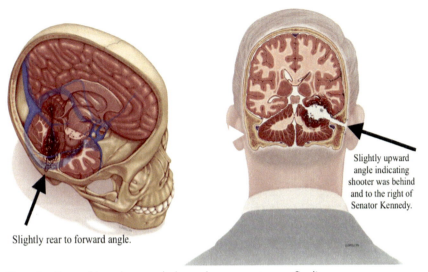

Slightly upward
angle indicating
shooter was behind
and to the right of
Senator Kennedy.

Slightly rear to forward angle.

Examination of head wounds based upon autopsy findings.

Sirhan Bashira Sirhan in custody immediately after shooting.

The authors have always felt that everyone in the kitchen pantry corridor prior to the shooting was put their deliberately.

Everyone in the room had to have received permission from someone in authority. In remarkable coincidence to John Kennedy's assassination, no cameras or professional film personnel were present when Robert Kennedy was brutally shot down from behind. Sirhan Sirhan will be further discussed in the 'Rats in the Woodpile' chapter and Thane Eugene Cesar in the 'Hail Cesar' chapter, but who else was in position and what might their roles have been?

There were numerous mysteries surrounding the assassination which included problems with the ballistics and forensics evidence and the possibility that multiple gunmen may have been present in the pantry of the hotel. According to the autopsy report, Kennedy was hit with three bullets and one bullet passed through his coat. Five other people were shot and injured, totaling nine shots. Sirhan's .22 caliber gun only held eight bullets so another person would have to be shooting as well, unless we are to believe that Sirhan was able to reload and fire again before Grier, Johnson, FBI Agent Barry or Plimpton could stop him. Within hours, FBI agent William Bailey found two additional bullets lodged in the pantry door frame. Police and FBI photographs show two more bullet holes in the pantry door divider and another hole in the jamb of a backstage door suggesting another four shots may have been fired. In 2005 Audio engineer, Philip Van Praag studied a sound recording of the shooting and made several discoveries. There were 13 shots with two instances of 'double shots,' fired so closely together they could not have come from the same gun. He also determined that five of the shots were from the opposite direction of Sirhan's supposed eight shots, suggesting they were fired from behind Robert Kennedy.

One person of interest became known as 'the lady in the polka dot dress.' Many eyewitnesses believe this woman was with Sirhan Sirhan and that she was using a form of mind control on him. From 1953 to 1973 the CIA was experimenting with an initiative known as 'MK-Ultra' reputed to be a form of mind control. MK-Ultra used numerous subjugated methods to manipulate its subject's mental states and brain functions, including the use of psychoactive drugs, especially LSD, without the subjects' consent through sensory deprivation, electroshock treatments and hypnosis. Over the 20-year period of MK-Ultra over 7,000 American veterans participated unwillingly in these programs at military bases, colleges and universities, hospitals, prisons, and pharmaceutical companies. Sirhan, under hypnosis, stated that upon cue from the girl in the polka dot dress that he went into 'range mode' believing he was at a firing range and seeing circles with targets in front of his eyes. "I thought that I was at the range more than I was actually shooting at any person, let alone Bobby Kennedy," Sirhan stated. He

5 December 1956

MEMORANDUM FOR: THE RECORD

SUBJECT: Project MKULTRA, Subproject 22

    1. The purpose of this project is to provide funds to carry out the isolation and characterization of the intoxicating substances present in certain varieties of Rivea corymbosa.

    2. ████████████████████ has conducted studies on this material which have lead to the development of methods which can now be applied to large samples of seed, thereby allowing the production of sufficient quantities of the active materials for definitive biological testing and characterization. ████████ has submitted the attached proposal to carry out this work as directed by TSS/████

    3. The Geschickter Fund for Medical Research, Inc., will serve as cutout for transfer of funds to the investigator. The estimated cost of the work is $5,950.00 for one year. To this must be added a four percent service charge for the Geschickter Fund, amounting to $238.00. Therefore, the total cost of this investigation for one year will not exceed $6,188.00.

    4. In accordance with the Memorandum...

Declassified CIA Document on MK-Ultra dated December 5, 1956.

Panel Finds CIA Broke Law.

CIA Infiltrated 17 Area Groups, Gave Out LSD

Suicide Revealed   **District the Focus**

Newspaper dated June 11, 1975 during Church Committee hearings.

remembered meeting the girl the night of the shooting and being attracted to her. Sirhan claims she was the person who led him to the pantry and that he had no plans of shooting anyone. He had been drinking Tom Collins cocktails earlier in the evening and after meeting the girl in the polka dot dress was going to have coffee with her. Sirhan claimed in the hypnotic interviews that the mystery girl touched or pinched him on the shoulder just before he spun around to see people coming through the pantry door. "Then I was on the target range...a flashback to the shooting range...I didn't know that I had a gun," Sirhan said to his attorney William Pepper. He also remembered seeing the flash of a second gun at the time of the shooting. This hypnotic state was recreated on Channel 4, in the U.K., in October 2011.

Hypnotist Derren Brown tested this theory on his TV show, 'The Experiments.' He took a highly hypnotizable subject and over a two-month period trained him to 'shoot and kill' a celebrity. The subject, however, did not know this was the experiment's goal. Brown gave his subject a two-part trigger that would send him into a hypnotic state: a polka dot pattern and a unique cell phone ring tone. When he saw this pattern and heard the tone, the young man was taught to touch his head to focus his concentration, and then fire a gun at a target on a range. But his final test occurred not at a range, but at a taping of British entertainer Stephen Fry's show. As the subject watched the show from a back row, a hidden camera showed a girl in a polka dot dress enter and sit in front of the subject. The cellphone rang. The girl turned to the subject and whispered, "The target is Stephen Fry." The subject hesitated a moment, then touched his forehead, opened the case, pulled out a gun loaded with blanks, stood, and fired. Stephen Fry, who was wired with squibs (the exploding fake blood packets used in movies to simulate gunshots), fell down 'dead.' The hypnotized man showed no reaction at the time. When shown a video of his act afterwards, the subject seemed genuinely surprised at what he had done. Brown's demonstration could be construed as definitive proof that hypnosis and mind control can effectively be used to program an assassin.

Sirhan's current attorney, William Pepper, recently had an expert hypnotize Sirhan in an open-ended fashion, during which Sirhan finally recalled that the touch of a girl in the pantry sent him into a mode where he thought he was firing at a target on a range. Could the girl in a polka dot dress eyewitness DiPierro saw 'holding' Sirhan moments before the shooting began have triggered his act?

Perhaps most significantly, by 1968 the CIA was thoroughly experienced and involved in various mind-control scenarios that involved drugs, hypnosis, and a combination of the two. One of the CIA's initial forays into this area came through a project code-named ARTICHOKE. One ARTICHOKE document proposed the question: "Can an individual ... be made to perform an act of attempted assassination involuntarily under the influence of ARTICHOKE?" This program eventually evolved into the MK-ULTRA program, an umbrella designation for hundreds of experiments that involved drugs, hypnosis, and biological and chemical warfare.

MEMORANDUM FOR THE RECORD

SUBJECT: Project ARTICHOKE

     ARTICHOKE is the Agency cryptonym for the study and/or use of "special" interrogation methods and techniques. These "special" interrogation methods have been known to include the use of drugs and chemicals, hypnosis, and "total isolation," a form of psychological harassment.

     A review of available file information obtained from Office of Security resources failed to reflect a comprehensive or complete picture of the ARTICHOKE program as participated in by the Office of Security. Fragmentary information contained in a variety of files previously maintained by the Security Research Staff (SRS) reflected several basic papers which described, in general terms, the program known as ARTICHOKE. Information contained therein indicated that prior to 1952, the Office of Security had studied the use of drugs and chemicals in "unconventional interrogation." These studies were evidently coordinated with the Agency unit which was then called OSI. OSI at that time apparently was the coordinating unit within CIA.

     One paper reflected that an Office of Security team as early as 1949-50 experimented with drugs and hypnosis under a project called BLUEBIRD. This paper also reflected that by 1951 actual interrogations utilizing drugs were conducted by a combined team of Office of Security and Office of Medical Services personnel, but few details were available.

Declassified CIA Document on Project ARTICHOKE.

There were numerous eyewitnesses that described Sirhan's actions in the pantry. Hotel assistant maitre'd Karl Uecker wrestled with Sirhan and said, "I told the authorities that Sirhan never got close enough for a point-blank shot—never." Eyewitness waiter Vincent DiPierro, 19, said in his statement, "When I first saw him (Sirhan) there was a girl behind him too. Very shapely, 21-24 years old, wearing a white dress with black or violet polka dots." Witnesses Darnell Johnson and George Green both said they saw a woman in a polka dot dress near Kennedy and that she fled the scene with another man after the shooting.

In all, 25 witnesses saw a woman in a polka dot dress. Thirteen claimed to see her with Sirhan moments before the shooting. Sergeant Paul Sharaga, the first police officer to arrive, said he spoke with the Bernstein's on the balcony outside the hotel's Embassy Room, "when a young couple, early 20's, came running from the direction of the Embassy Room shouting, "We shot him, we shot Kennedy."

Sandy Serrano, 20, also claimed she saw the same woman claiming they shot Kennedy. Initial police reports claimed she recanted her story two weeks later; Serrano denies she ever made this statement. "There was a lot of badgering that was going on," she said, "I said what the police wanted me to say. I was interrogated for hours with polka dot dresses all around me. It was just a bad scene." She said, "the investigators badgered me into changing my story."

Records of the case prove that the Los Angeles police investigators bullied and badgered eyewitnesses to change their statements regarding the number of shots and who reported conspirators leaving the scene. While Sirhan's case was still being appealed the LAPD also inexplicably and illegally destroyed thousands of pieces of evidence, including 2,410 photographs of the crime scene before and after the shooting as well as the door frames and ceiling tiles in the pantry that held vital ballistics evidence. Also missing from the files were taped statements of 51 key witnesses, including 29 with accounts that related directly to questions involving conspiracy. The LAPD also threatened eyewitnesses who claimed they saw Thane Eugene Cesar, a hotel security guard, draw and shoot his gun. This was the same security guard that after RFK was shot, he turned and tore off Cesar's clip-on tie.

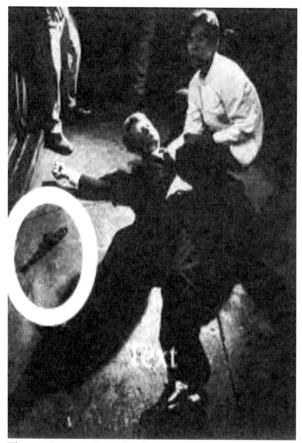

Thane Eugene Cesar's clip-on tie.

The two LAPD officers in charge of the investigation were connected with the CIA. The LAPD was working closely with the CIA on their Operation Chaos program in the late 1960's. This CIA initiative included domestic surveillance to target anti-war and civil rights activists. Witnesses who gave conflicting accounts of the official story of Sirhan as the lone assassin were either given coercive polygraph examinations by LAPD Sergeant Enrique Hernandez or their testimony was conveniently ignored, similar to what happened to witnesses with the Warren Commission Report on JFK. In addition to Hernandez, LAPD officer Manuel Pena was in charge of signing off on every report and deciding which leads to follow and who to interview. Both men had trained as police officers in South America for the CIA connected Office of Public Safety. According to FBI agent Roger La Jeunesse, Pena had performed assignments for the CIA for more than a decade. (b)

Interior view of Ambassador.

Scene from Pretty Woman, note columns.

The grand majesty of the Ambassador Hotel began to decline immediately after Robert Kennedy's assassination. The area saw a surge of gang activity, poverty, and an influx of illegal drugs. The hotel closed to guests in 1989 but remained opened for filming and private events. Privately, it became known as Ambassador Studios. Fittingly, six Academy Award shows were held at the Ambassador. Although the exterior shots were of The Beverly Wilshire in Beverly Hills, 1990's, 'Pretty Woman' interior lobby and elevator scenes were shot at the Ambassador. The fountain in the middle of the Ambassador lobby is clearly visible in the background of the elevator scenes. Another movie containing scenes shot within the Ambassador is Arnold Schwarzenegger's 1994, 'True Lies.'

The hotel was host to a staggering list of Hollywood legends, heads of state, and Presidents. Hoover, Roosevelt, Truman, Eisenhower, Kennedy, Johnson, and Nixon, essentially every President from 1929-1974. Soviet Premier Nikita Khrushchev stayed there in 1959. Ronald Reagan used the Ambassador to announce his bid for Governor of California. Marilyn Monroe started her modeling career as a client of the poolside modeling agency, Blue Book Models. Howard Hughes and Jean Harlow made the Ambassador their home for years. Bing Crosby and Barbra Streisand had their start at the Ambassador. The hotel's Cocoanut Grove was the hot spot to see Gene Kelly, Diana Ross, Judy Garland, Louis Armstrong and Nat King Cole. Julie Andrews and numerous other celebrities and entertainers all played the Grove.

Ambassador Hotel and pool circa 1964.

In 1989, after 68 years of service, the Ambassador officially closed primarily due to lack of funds necessary to bring the hotel up to current Fire Code requirements. The Los Angeles Unified School District (LAUSD) officially took ownership of the hotel in 2001 after purchasing the property for $76.5 million. The Ambassador was officially demolished in 2005 and a new high school was built in its place. Ironic that history was destroyed so an alternative and false history could be taught.

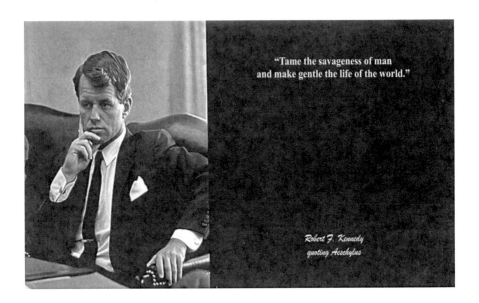

"Tame the savageness of man
and make gentle the life of the world."

Robert F. Kennedy
quoting Aeschylus

Six

<u>Rats In The Woodpile</u>

Sirhan Bishara Sirhan was born in Mandatory Palestine, Jerusalem on March 19, 1944. His family immigrated to the United States, residing briefly in New York and then moving to California when he was 12 years old.

Like Lee Harvey Oswald, five years prior with John F. Kennedy, Sirhan Bishara Sirhan is 100% innocent in the killing of Robert F. Kennedy. The only difference is Sirhan lived to stand trial and was not eliminated by the powers that be, primarily because he was hypnotized into shooting at RFK and did not remember any of his actions the night of RFK's assassination. On June 9, 1968, while in police custody, he admitted guilt in a recorded confession.

At Sirhan's trial, his lawyers made a motion in chambers to enter a plea of guilty to first-degree murder in exchange for life imprisonment versus the death penalty. Sirhan informed Judge Herbert Walker that he wanted to withdraw his not guilty plea and plead guilty as charged on all counts. The court denied this motion. He also asked for his lawyers to recuse themselves from his case. Judge Walker also denied this request. His counsel entered another motion to withdraw from the case of their own volition, but that request was denied as well.

Opening statements began on February 12, 1969. The lead prosecutor in the case was Lynn 'Buck' Compton. The prosecution's case was based on witnesses seeing Sirhan at the

Ambassador Hotel two nights before the attack, and the fact that he visited a gun range the day before. The prosecution team also presented Sirhan's garbage collector, Alvin Clark, who testified that Sirhan had told him in May, 1968 that he intended to shoot Robert Kennedy when he came to Los Angeles. Sirhan's defense counsel proposed that he was mentally deficient. This motion failed when the prosecuting team produced handwritten testimony from Sirhan stating, "RFK must die," written over 1000 times, along with other threatening remarks.

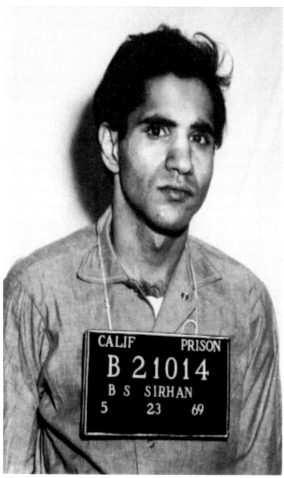

Mugshot of Sirhan Bishara Sirhan.

Sirhan's incompetent defense team never challenged the prosecution teams inconsistencies. His primary attorney, Grant Cooper, was facing criminal charges in another case for lying about the source of stolen grand jury transcripts on behalf of mob boss Johnny Roselli, who was instrumental in the CIA's Castro assassination attempt. From the outset, Cooper bullied Sirhan into admitting guilt to save him from the death penalty and actively blocked the inclusion of ballistics and other evidence that may have proven Sirhan innocent. LAPD criminalist DeWayne Wolfer mislabeled and misrepresented the bullet and gun evidence to the Grand Jury at trial. The bullet in question was recovered from Kennedy's neck and was never matched to Sirhan's gun. The test bullets Wolfer presented at trial were not from Sirhan's gun, (Serial #H53725) but from a different gun taken from an LAPD evidence locker (#H18602). Once more, Sirhan's defense attorney Cooper offered no challenge to this blatantly false and misleading evidence.

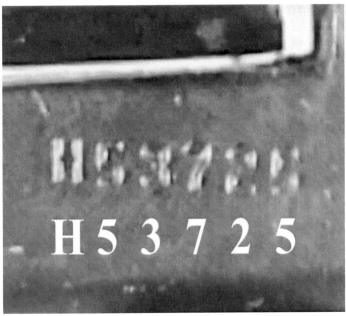

Photo of Serial number H53725 of Sirhan's gun.

123

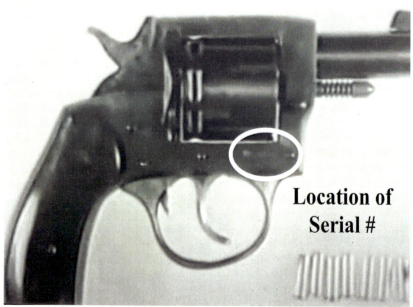

Location of
Serial #

Location of Serial #H53725 as noted on previous page.

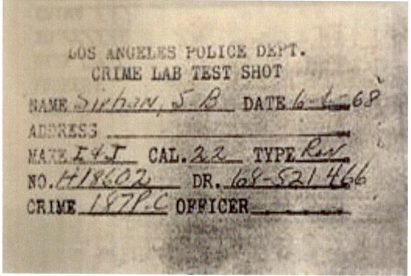

LOS ANGELES POLICE DEPT.
CRIME LAB TEST SHOT

NAME *Sirhan, S B* DATE *6-4-68*
ADDRESS _____
MAKE *I&J* CAL. *22* TYPE *Rev*
NO. *H18602* DR. *68-521 466*
CRIME *187 P.C* OFFICER _____

Crime Lab report of Serial #H18602, notating different gun.

On April 17, 1969, Sirhan was convicted of Robert F. Kennedy's death and six days later sentenced to die in the California gas chamber. In February 1972, his sentence was commuted to life in prison when California overturned the death penalty case in 'People v. Anderson.'

Sirhan was also denied another trial on appeal and has had numerous parole hearings. In 1982, he told the parole board, "I sincerely believe that if Robert Kennedy were alive today, I believe he would not countenance singling me out for this kind of treatment. I think he would be among the first to say that, however horrible the deed I committed 14 years ago was, that it should not be the cause for denying me equal treatment under the laws of this country." At his 15th parole hearing in 2016, Paul Schrade, 91, himself a victim of Sirhan's shooting testified by saying, "a second shooter killed Kennedy and that Sirhan was intended to be a distraction from the real gunman by an unknown conspiracy." Again, Sirhan was denied parole. On August 27, 2021, his 16th appearance before the parole board, they voted to grant Sirhan parole, concluding that he no longer posed a threat to society. He had been incarcerated for over 53 years. This decision was subject to a 90-day review by the California Board of Parole Hearings after which Governor Gavin Newsom had 30 days to grant, reverse, or modify the decision. Of course, the Board's decision was reversed and Sirhan remains in custody. Two of Robert Kennedy's sons, Douglas and Robert Jr. both supported Sirhan's release. Robert Kennedy Jr. stated, "The pain that we all feel from my father's death should not prevent us from pursuit of the truth. I firmly believe the idea that Sirhan murdered my dad is a fiction that is impeding justice." The following letter was written to the Board of Parole Hearings from Robert Kennedy Jr.

Board of Parole Hearings

Dept. of Corrections and Rehabilitation

August 27, 2021

This evening I learned that the Los Angeles Sheriff's Department late today submitted a letter opposing Mr. Sirhan's release "on behalf of the Kennedy family." Please know that that letter was not at the direction of the "family", and certainly not me.

As you may know, I have been a strong advocate for the release of Mr. Sirhan B. Sirhan since I learned of evidence that was not presented to the court during his trial. After years of careful investigation, I arrived at the conviction that the story of my father's murder was not as cut and dried as portrayed at trial. While Sirhan clearly fired shots at my father, overwhelming evidence suggests that these were not the shots that took his life. I also understand that Sirhan's guilt or innocence is not an issue in this proceeding. I sought to meet with Mr. Sirhan and we spent several hours together. During that meeting I was impressed by the genuineness of his remorse for the indisputable part he played in my father's assassination. Sirhan wept, clenched my hands, and asked for forgiveness from me, from my siblings, and from my mother for his part in that tragic evening's events.

My father taught me to believe in redemption and justice. His favorite quote from Aeschylus, urged that we should

"Tame the savageness of man and make gentle the life of the world." In my own life I have experienced the miracles of redemption and forgiveness. I believe that Mr. Sirhan is redeemed. At 77, he is a gentle, humble, kindhearted, frail, and harmless old man who poses no threat to our community. His release will be testimony to the humanity, compassion, and idealism of our justice system to which my father devoted his life.

While nobody can speak definitively on behalf of my father, I firmly believe that, based on his consuming commitment to fairness and justice, that he would strongly encourage this Board to release Mr. Sirhan because of Sirhan's impressive record of rehabilitation. This action would be consistent with the rule of law, which requires Sirhan's release absent evidence that he currently poses a danger.

Mr. Sirhan was sentenced to life with the possibility of parole. Parole is the rule and denial are an exception only be justified if the Board determines that Mr. Sirhan still presents a high risk of danger to the community. I understand that Mr. Sirhan has more than rehabilitated himself. I further understand that his most recent risk assessment performed by CDCR psychologists has confirmed the many prior risk assessments which opine that Mr. Sirhan does not pose a high risk of danger to society.

Should he be released, I offer to be a guiding friend to him. I know that Paul Schrade has made the same offer to Mr. Sirhan.

Any opposition to Mr. Sirhan's release, simply based on the crime is contrary to the law and contrary to the concepts of redemption and forgiveness. I ask that you extend the same consideration to Mr. Sirhan that you give to other "lifers" who have been convicted of murder and of whom you have released.

Sincerely,
Robert F. Kennedy. Jr.

"With Gov. Newsom's decision to overrule Sirhan's parole, is just one more California official who claims to love my father but persists in denying him justice," stated Robert Kennedy Jr.

This letter was written after Robert Kennedy Jr. personally traveled to the Richard J. Donovan Correctional Center to confront Sirhan Sirhan, the man convicted for killing his father. The meeting took place on December 19, 2018 with Laurie Dusek, one of Sirhan's defense attorneys. RFK Jr. had reached out to Dusek to set the meeting up because he was convinced that Sirhan Sirhan was, "the wrong person convicted of killing his father" according to Dusek. She continued, "they (Donovan Correctional facility) only admitted him (RFK Jr.) to the prison because we said he was an attorney interested in joining Sirhan's legal team."

After the two men shook hands, Sirhan immediately expressed, "the shame he felt for being associated with his father's assassination." RFK Jr. replied, "I KNOW you didn't kill my father." RFK Jr. had spoken many times with his Father's top aide Paul Schrade. He had seen the Coroner's report stating that several shots, including the fatal shot had come from behind, and

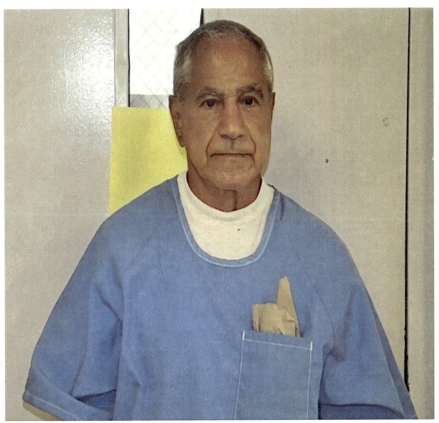

Sirhan at Donovan Correctional Facility December 18, 2019.

he had listened to audio recordings from the night of the shootings. He was sure in his belief that Sirhan was not his Father's killer.

"It took a lot of courage for RFK to go there," said Dusek following the nearly three-hour meeting. She continued, "At first, there was nervousness, but as they got used to each other, RFK Jr. expressed genuine interest in Sirhan's welfare and daily life."

In an article RFK Jr. wrote for the San Francisco Chronicle describing the meeting between himself and Sirhan he stated, "I was impressed with the genuineness of Sirhan's remorse for his role in my father's shooting." RFK continued, "Sirhan wept, clenched my hands and asked for forgiveness from me, from my siblings and from my mother for his part in the tragedy. At 77, he seems gentle, humble, kindhearted, frail and harmless." (a)

Mary Muhzea Sirhan at her son's trial.

In his 2018 documentary film, 'The Second Dallas,' filmmaker Massimo Mazzucco interviewed Sirhan's mother, Mary Muhzea Sirhan, regarding Sirhan's actions. The narrative of which she speaks is very similar to Marguerite Oswald defending her son, Lee. She asked, "Son, tell me, why would you do that? (kill Robert Kennedy). Sirhan replied to his mother, "I'm sorry, I do not remember anything...I was told that I killed Senator Robert Kennedy."

The question now becomes, if Sirhan was not guilty of killing Robert Kennedy, who else had the means, motive, and opportunity to eliminate him? Two names that immediately surface are David Sanchez Morales and George Joannides. Of great interest, both CIA files on these gentlemen are still unavailable nearly 33 years after Joannides death and 45 years after Morales'. David Morales had told friends, "I was in Dallas when we got the Son of a Bitch, and I was in Los Angeles when we got the little Bastard." (b)

David Morales

What was the background of David Sanchez Morales? He joined the Army in 1946 and served in the 82nd Airborne, an infantry division specializing in parachute assault operations into denied areas. It is also the Presidential bodyguard division. How convenient. Under cover of the U.S. Army, Morales joined the CIA in 1951 and became an operative for the CIA's Directorate for Plans, specifically the Executive Action project. The EA project was implemented to kill foreign leaders deemed uncooperative to the United States. Morales was involved in Operation PBSUCCESS, the CIA covert operation that overthrew the democratically elected President of Guatemala, Jacobo Arbenz Guzman. He was also involved in the capture of Che Guevara and the overthrow of Chilean President Salvador Allende.

During the 1960's Morales was also heavily involved with JM/WAVE, the code name for a secret United States covert operations and intelligence gathering station operated by the CIA from 1961-1968. This operation was based twelve miles south of the main campus of the University of Miami. It has also been referred to as 'Miami or Wave Station.' JMWAVE's first plan was the implementation of 'Operation Mongoose,' a U.S. effort to overthrow Cuban President Fidel Castro. They were also active in the Bay of Pigs invasion and the Cuban Missile Crisis. JMWAVE

JMWAVE Buildings, circa 1961.

operated after the Cuban Missile Crisis under the leadership of Ted Shackley (Bureau Chief, Miami) and became the largest CIA station in the world outside of CIA headquarters in Langley,

Virginia, and had a budget of $50 million in 1962 ($450 million in 2023). The Miami operation had over 400 CIA agents or informants and an estimated 15,000 anti-Castro Cuban exiles on its payroll. 300 to 400 'front companies' were created as 'safe houses' for operative training and housing. They performed

Bradley Ayers

nonstop espionage, sabotage, and were planning another invasion of Cuba.

Working with Morales at JMWAVE and Operation Mongoose was Bradley Ayers. Ayers, also with the CIA, was part of Special Group Augmented (SGA) through his connection with William King Harvey. Ayers even suggested that Robert Kennedy visited CIA personnel at the Miami station. "I'm confident in my gut, that Bobby Kennedy was aware of what we were doing down there. It wasn't a case of the Agency (CIA) mounting these assassination operations without the knowledge of the SGA...RFK had a hands-on kind of control of the operations." Ayers was interviewed by Jeremy Gunn of the Assassination Records Review Board in May, 1995. According to Gunn, "Ayers claims to have found in the course of his private investigative work, a credible witness who can put David Morales inside the Ambassador Hotel in Los Angeles on the night Robert Kennedy was assassinated."

OFFICE OF THE SECRETARY OF DEFENSE
WASHINGTON 25, D.C.

20 February 1962

EYES ONLY OF ADDRESSEES

FROM: Brig. Gen. Lansdale *Ed*

SUBJECT: The Cuba Project

      Transmitted herewith is the projection of actions to help
Cubans recapture their freedom. This total plan is EYES ONLY.
The lives of many brave people depend on the security of this
paper entrusted to you. Any inference that this plan exists could
place the President of the United States in a most damaging position.

      This is a specific plan, with time phases. It responds to
the request of the Special Group (5412) for such a paper. I urge
that this paper not be made known, in this complete form, beyond
yourself and those named as addressees.

      The Attorney General
      Special Group: General Taylor
      State: Secretary Rusk, Alexis Johnson, Richard Goodwin
      Defense: Secretary McNamara, Deputy Secretary Gilpatric,
             Brig. Gen. Craig   *Gen. Lemnitzer*
      CIA: John McCone, Richard Helms, William Harvey
      USIA: Ed Murrow, Don Wilson
      White House: President · Bundy

SGA, note AG Kennedy and CIA's McCone, Helms & Harvey.

SENSITIVE

20 February 1962

Program Review
by Brig. Gen. Lansdale

THE CUBA PROJECT

The Goal. In keeping with the spirit of the Presidential memorandum
of 30 November 1961, the United States will help the people of Cuba overthrow the Communist regime from within Cuba and institute a new government with which the United States can live in peace.

The Situation.   We still know too little about the real situation inside
Cuba, although we are taking energetic steps to learn more. However,
some salient facts are known. It is known that the Communist regime is
an active Sino-Soviet spearhead in our Hemisphere and that Communist
controls inside Cuba are severe. Also, there is evidence that the repres-
sive measures of the Communists, together with disappointments in
Castro's economic dependency on the Communist formula, have resulted
in an anti-regime atmosphere among the Cuban people which makes a
resistance program a distinct and present possibility.

Time is running against us. The Cuban people feel helpless and are
losing hope fast. They need symbols of inside resistance and of outside
interest soon. They need something they can join with the hope of starting
to work surely towards overthrowing the regime. Since late November, we
have been working hard to re-orient the operational concepts within the U.S.
government and to develop the hard intelligence and operational assets
required for success in our task.

The next National Intelligence Estimate on Cuba (NIE 85-62) promises
to be a useful document dealing with our practical needs and with due
recognition of the sparsity of hard facts. The needs of the Cuba project,
as it goes into operation, plus the increasing U.S. capability for intelligence
collection, should permit more frequent estimates for our guidance. These
will be prepared on a periodic basis.

Premise of Action.   Americans once ran a successful revolution. It
was run from within, and succeeded because there was timely and strong
political, economic, and military help by nations outside who supported
our cause. Using this same concept of revolution from within, we must
now help the Cuban people to stamp out tyranny and gain their liberty.

On 18 January, the Chief of Operations assigned thirty-two tasks to
Departments and Agencies of the U.S. government, in order to provide
a realistic assessment and preparation of U.S. capabilities. The Attorney
General and the Special Group were apprised of this action. The answers
received on 15 February provided the basis for planning a realistic course
of action. The answers also revealed that the course of action must contain continuing coordination and firm overall guidance.

The course of action set forth herein is realistic within present operational estimates and intelligence. Actually, it represents the maximum
target timing which the operational people jointly considered feasible. It
aims for a revolt which can take place in Cuba by October 1962. It is a

SENSITIVE

This document contains ___ pgs.

Copy No. _1_ of _12_ copies.

series of target actions and dates, not a rigid time-table. The target dates are timed as follows:

Phase I, Action, March 1962. Start moving in.

Phase II, Build-up, April-July 1962. Activating the necessary opera- tions inside Cuba for revolution and concurrently applying the vital political, economic, and military-type support from outside Cuba.

Phase III, Readiness, 1 August 1962, check for final policy decision.

Phase IV, Resistance, August-September 1962, move into guerrilla operations.

Phase V, Revolt, first two weeks of October 1962. Open revolt and overthrow of the Communist regime.

Phase VI, Final, during month of October 1962. Establishment of new government.

Plan of Action. Attached is an operational plan for the overthrow of the Communist regime in Cuba, by Cubans from within Cuba, with outside help from the U.S. and elsewhere. Since this is an operation to prompt and support a revolt by the people in a Communist police state, flexibility is a must for success. Decisions on operational flexibility rest with the Chief of Operations, with consultation in the Special Group when policy matters are involved. Target actions and dates are detailed in the attached operational plans, which cover:

A. Basic Action Plan Inside Cuba

B. Political Support Plan

C. Economic Support Plan

D. Psychological Support Plan

E. Military Support Plan

F. Sabotage Support Plan

G. Intelligence Support Plan

Early Policy Decisions. The operational plan for clandestine U.S. support of a Cuban movement inside Cuba to overthrow the Communist regime is within policy limits already set by the President. A vital decision, still to be made, is on the use of open U.S. force to aid the Cuban people in winning their liberty. If conditions and assets permitting a revolt are achieved in Cuba, and if U.S. help is required to sustain this condition, will the U.S. respond promptly with military force to aid the Cuban revolt? The contingencies under which such military deployment would be needed, and recommended U.S. responses, are detailed in a memorandum being prepared by the Secretaries of State and of Defense. An early decision is required, prior to deep involvement of the Cubans in this program.

TOP SECRET

SENSITIVE

Distribution:

Copy No.

1. The President

2. The Attorney General

3. General Taylor

4. The Secretary of State
   (through Deputy Under Secretary Johnson)

5. The Secretary of Defense
   (through Deputy Secretary Gilpatric)

6. The Director, Central Intelligence Agency

7. The Director, U. S. Information Agency
   (through Deputy Director Wilson)

8. State (Mr. Goodwin)

9. Defense (Brig. Gen. Craig)

10. CIA (Mr. Harvey)

11.-12. Chief of Operations (Brig. Gen. Lansdale)

SENSITIVE

TOP SECRET

3

Robert Maheu, FBI, questioned after leaving courtroom.

Johnny Roselli

The CIA's intelligence gathering station in Miami, JM/WAVE was established as the operations center for Task Force W, the CIA's unit dedicated to Operation Mongoose. The CIA enlisted the Mafia, who were eager to regain their Cuban casino operations and to plot an assassination attempt on Castro. William King Harvey was the CIA case officer who dealt directly with Mafia soldier Johnny Roselli. Roselli was introduced to the CIA by former FBI Agent Robert Mahue. Mahue knew Roselli and was aware of his connection to the gambling syndicate in Cuba prior to Castro's takeover. The gambling syndicate operation began in May 1961 with Project ZR/RIFLE, also headed by William King Harvey. This scheme contained "an Executive Action Capability (assassination of foreign leaders), a general stand-by capability to carry out assassinations when required." Project ZR/RIFLE's main purpose was to identify potential agents and research assassination techniques that could be utilized. Project ZR/RIFLE and the CIA's operation in Cuba was bolstered when Harvey became the head of the task force in Cuba. Roselli was tasked with recruiting Cubans from Florida to help with Castro's assassination. (c)

"Executive Action" was a CIA euphemism, defined as a project for research into developing means for overthrowing foreign political leaders, including a "capability to perform assassinations." (Harvey, 6/25/75, p. 34) Bissell indicated that Executive Action covered a "wide spectrum of actions" to "eliminate the effectiveness" of foreign leaders, with assassination as the "most extreme" action in the spectrum. (Bissell, 7/22/75, p. 32) The Inspector General's Report described executive action as a "general standby capability" to carry out assassination when required. (I.G. Report, p. 37) The project was given the code name ZR/RIFLE by the CIA.[1]

Excerpt from HSCA Report describing "Executive Action" (ZR/RIFLE).

David Talbot's, 'Brothers: The Hidden History of the Kennedy Years,' identifies former FBI agent and the CIA's Castro assassination plot coordinator, Robert Maheu, as the likely planner of Robert Kennedy's assassination. Multiple government documents prove that Maheu was working on assassination plots for both the CIA and FBI in assassination plots in the 1960's. Maheu also admitted to Talbot that he hated the Kennedy's. (d). Joining Morales and Ayers in Miami was George Joannides. Joannides joined the CIA in 1952, but by 1963 was Chief of the Psychological Warfare branch at the Miami station. Although primarily considered a possible assassin for JFK, his motive and clandestine nature cannot be cavalierly dismissed. In 1978, the CIA talked Joannides out of retirement to serve as their liaison to the House Select Committee on Assassinations. To no one's surprise, Joannides revealed nothing regarding his involvement with the Pro-Castro group or his relationship with Lee Harvey Oswald. After discovering Joannides previous CIA positions, G. Robert Blakey stated later that Joannides should have been charged with obstruction of justice to the Congress. In July 1981, the CIA awarded the Career Intelligence Medal to Joannides.

Joannides (L) accepting CIA's Career Intelligence Medal.

The United States of America

Central Intelligence Agency

Citation

MR. GEORGE E. JOANNIDES

is hereby awarded the

CAREER INTELLIGENCE MEDAL

in recognition of his exceptional achievement with the Central Intelligence Agency for more than twenty-eight years. During that period, he served in diverse assignments of increasing responsibility at Headquarters, the domestic field, and overseas. His outstanding linguistic skills and area knowledge, expertise in a specialized operational activity, and superb mangerial techniques truly earned him the respect and admiration of superiors and colleagues. Mr. Joannides' overall career performance and dedication to duty uphold the highest traditions of the Operations Directorate, reflecting credit on himself and the Federal service.

Joannides is Awarded the Career Intelligence Medal for 'stonewalling' HSCA investigation into JFK assassination.

During the HSCA hearings in 1978, the CIA acknowledged it has more than 50 classified documents regarding Joannides's actions in 1963 that are still being held based upon 'National Security.'

This chapter would not be complete without mentioning the largest rat in the woodpile, the U.S. media. The media has been influenced by the CIA since the intelligence agency's inception in 1947. Knowing that ballistics would prove that there were at least 13, possibly 14 shots from Sirhan's eight-shot revolver, the LAPD, FBI, and CIA all knew they had a problem. Just like they did in Dallas 4½ years earlier, the government fearlessly trotted out their preposterous 'magic bullets' theory once again. Only this time, there would be three bullets instead of one. To account for one of the extra bullets, the FBI (with CIA influence) said that the bullet that went directly through RFK's suit without hitting him also went into the ceiling tile. This would appear logical except for the fact that not one witnesses could place Sirhan standing behind RFK. They then claimed this bullet didn't go into the ceiling tile at all but struck victim Paul Schrade. This is a true magic bullet when you consider where all three men were standing.

In order for this theory to work, Sirhan needed to be on his knees behind RFK, shoot upwards through the jacket without hitting him and then strike Schrade. However, the angle of injury for Schrade would have to place him approximately four feet higher than Kennedy. Once more, the rats in the CIA knew this wouldn't pass the smell test. However, they were not ready to eliminate the possibility of the same shot going through Bobby's jacket into the forehead of Paul Schrade. Onto diagram two.

Diagram one showing where Sirhan, RFK, and Schrade had to be located in order for their first 'magic bullet' to hit both Kennedy and Schrade.

In this magic bullet theory (#2), the bullet is fired from Sirhan through Kennedy and only penetrates his jacket. This is a shot from behind traveling upwards on a right to left trajectory. The bullet then dives to the floor, reverses direction, and goes up and to the right hitting Schrade in the forehead. Not moving away from another magic bullet (#3), this bullet deflects off of the ceiling tile, hits the floor, and then ricochets into Elizabeth Evans, as she is bending down to avoid gunfire, also striking her in the forehead. Other magic bullets are allegedly passing through two victims and lodging into various door frames, although no bullet fragments were ever located in the door frames. This is why the LAPD had to conveniently remove the

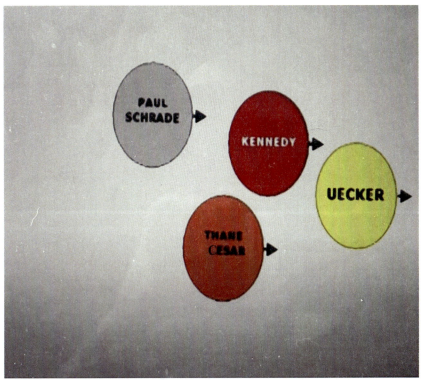

Position of each man as they passed through the kitchen pantry.

door frames and ceiling tiles and destroy them <u>before</u> the trial of Sirhan started. All of these magic bullets are irrelevant, since Sirhan's attorneys never argued the ballistic evidence and were only interested in providing Sirhan's admission of guilt to prevent the death penalty. They never argued there was another gunman present in the pantry despite overwhelming ballistic evidence.

As they did regarding the John F. Kennedy assassination, LIFE magazine would once again misrepresent the facts. The infamous photos taken by Boris Yaro was edited for the cover of LIFE magazine in order to obfuscate the facts. Incredibly, critical evidence of another shooter behind Robert Kennedy (Thane Eugene Cesar) was manipulated for the cover. As he was falling from his wounds, Robert Kennedy pulled the clip-on tie from Cesar, perhaps as a reactionary instinct after being shot from behind. In the Yaro's photos, you clearly see the clip-on tie

Thane Eugene Cesar photograph without clip-on tie.

next to Robert Kennedy. However, in the LIFE magazine cover, it has been airbrushed out. A minor detail, but if the image were printed with the tie, logically the American people would be asking, "who's tie is this?" In the Turner/Christian book, 'The Assassination of Robert F. Kennedy,' there is a photograph (above) taken of Cesar after the assassination without his tie attached. If the American people were given this information in 1968, they would have immediately asked, "why is this security guard's tie lying next to Senator Kennedy and who is this guy?"

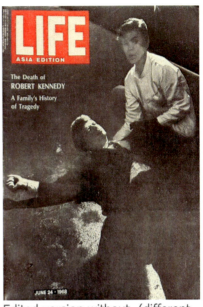

Original photo with clip-on tie.   Edited version without. (different photo, same time period)

When one considers a possible conspiracy in RFK's murder, thought should be given to what organizations may have wanted him dead and what they stood to gain with RFK out of the way. At the front of the line? The American Military Industrial Complex, the CIA, and Texas Big Oil, all of whom were realizing unimaginable profits thanks to the Vietnam War. Had RFK gained the White House, the cash cow for all three would disappear, the war would end, tens of thousands of American lives would be saved and the CIA's position as a major power in world intelligence would be severely compromised, since RFK was convinced of their involvement in his Brother's murder. Next, the Mafia – incensed that Joe Kennedy Sr.'s promise to give them unchecked access to The White House once JFK was elected had gone unrealized and that RFK, acting as JFK's AG was relentlessly prosecuting Mafia chieftains. Next the FBI. Although LBJ had given his neighbor and buddy J. Edgar Hoover the title of Director for Life, Hoover knew his tenure would be threatened had RFK become President. Lastly, the American media acting as CIA spokesmen for years once their vicious lies were exposed.

The authors feel very strongly that the same sinister cabal of individuals and rogue agents within various U.S. government agencies were responsible for murdering both Kennedy Brothers, in some cases to preserve their very existence.

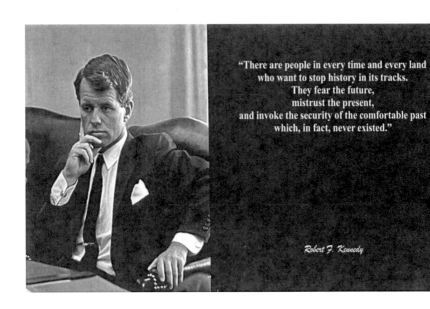

"There are people in every time and every land who want to stop history in its tracks. They fear the future, mistrust the present, and invoke the security of the comfortable past which, in fact, never existed."

Robert F. Kennedy

Seven

<u>Hail Cesar</u>

Unlike his brother before him, Robert Kennedy's assassination has not received nearly as much scrutiny as warranted. Anyone who has read William Turner and John Christian's, 'The Assassination of Robert F. Kennedy—A Searching Look at the Conspiracy and Cover-Up 1968-1978,' or Philip Melanson's, 'The Robert F. Kennedy Assassination—New Revelations on the Conspiracy and Cover-Up 1968-1991,' knows with absolute certainty that RFK was killed by a CIA contract agent/security guard, Thane Eugene Cesar. The ballistics evidence alone proves this. (a/b)

The official government version of the RFK assassination is eerily similar to JFK's, both claiming that one lone assassin fired all the shots and neither event involved a conspiracy. The thoroughly fabricated version of Robert F. Kennedy's assassination was corroborated by the LAPD, the LA District Attorney's office and the FBI. Sirhan B. Sirhan was one of approximately 77 persons in the Ambassador pantry waiting for RFK to walk through on his way to a press conference in the Colonial Room. Sirhan, never closer than 4-5' in front of RFK, pulled his eight-shot, .22 caliber revolver and began firing. After the first two shots, his arm and gun were secured by Rosey Grier, wrestling him against a table, and pointing the gun away from the Senator. It is believed that one of these first two shots hit Paul Schrade. The other six shots were fired randomly and hit four other bystanders. Those five victims sustained non-life-threatening injuries. Every eyewitness who testified stated that

Sirhan was always in front of Kennedy and was never closer than four feet away. However, RFK's wounds were all from the rear and upward, clearing indicating more than one shooter. RFK sustained four separate wounds. One bullet lodged in his spine near the neck, another bullet entered his back and exited his chest, the fatal bullet entered the back of his head just behind his right ear, lodging in his brain. A fourth bullet passed harmlessly through his clothing. Here lies the first major problem with ballistics, nine shots supposedly being fired from an eight-shot revolver, four shots striking RFK and five shots injuring five other victims. The only other person in the pantry who had a gun was the armed security guard standing directly behind and to the right of Senator Kennedy, Thane Eugene Cesar.

Thane Eugene Cesar

Unlike JFK, Robert Kennedy was immediately given a meticulous autopsy. The Medical Examiner who performed the procedure, Dr. Thomas Noguchi, stated that all of RFK's wounds were fired from behind the Senator with the fatal shot fired 1" behind his right ear, no further than 3" away. He added that there were powder burns consistent with a muzzle shot fired at point blank range, known as a 'tap.' Sirhan was never behind Senator Kennedy. With absolute certainly, Cesar, holding the only other gun in the room, was. The subsequent investigation by the LAPD was at best questionable if not completely suspect. Suspicious circumstances were intentionally ignored. Leads were not pursued. People who had acted suspiciously before RFK's acceptance speech were never questioned or identified. Credible witnesses who gave testimony suggesting the presence of conspirators in the pantry were coerced into changing their accounts as to what happened. Questionable statements provided by others were accepted as truth as long as they implicated a lone shooter. Sworn affidavits were altered. Over 3,400 witness interview tape recordings were destroyed. Police evidence logs were falsified. Crime lab experts tampered with evidence, altered test results, and gave false testimony. 2,410 photographs were destroyed or burned. The doorways and ceiling panels within the Ambassador pantry were destroyed, eliminating evidence of additional bullets being fired. (Suspiciously familiar to the manner in which JFK's limousine was illegally confiscated by the Secret Service immediately after he was assassinated, in order to conceal potentially damning evidence.) The LAPD crime lab could not exclusively match any of the recovered bullets to Sirhan's gun. Alarmingly, during Sirhan's trial, Judge Herbert Van Walker threw out any evidence that supported anything other than a lone gunman theory. Researchers have always suspected the CIA was involved in or orchestrated the LAPD cover-up. Of note, LAPD Lt. Manuel S.

Pena, who was the head of the special police unit responsible for investigating RFK's assassination was a known CIA operative or asset.

In her 2018 book, 'A Lie Too Big to Fail,' author Lisa Pease also believes that RFK's assassination was the result of a conspiracy orchestrated by Robert Maheu and undercover operatives of the CIA's covert actions division. Maheu was an ex-FBI agent and an ex-CIA employee with ties to the highest and most secretive levels of the CIA. He continued to perform illegal tasks for the CIA after he left the agency. Maheu was instrumental in recruiting mafia boss Johnny Roselli and others to help overthrow Fidel Castro in the early 1960's. His connections to the underworld and CIA are legendary. (c)

Thane Eugene Cesar (circled in red) moments before escorting RFK.

Thane Eugene Cesar's full-time job/cover was as a maintenance plumber at the Lockheed Aircraft plant in Burbank. This position required a security clearance from the Department of Defense. A co-worker of Cesar's at Lockheed told researchers Turner and Christian that the plant was a CIA controlled U-2 spy plane facility, and that Cesar often worked in a restricted area that only special personnel had access to. At the time of RFK's assassination, Cesar had been employed as a security guard for Ace Guard Service, where he had worked for one day only the previous week. Cesar was intentionally placed by the CIA to escort Robert Kennedy through the pantry to the planned press conference, away from television and reporter's cameras. When Sirhan drew his gun, according to his own statement Cesar drew his handgun as well. Witnesses collaborated his testimony and one witness, reporter Don Schulman, claimed that Cesar fired his gun at least once. In a complete and alarming breach of normal police procedure, the LAPD chose not examine Cesar's pistol. Although he owned a .22 caliber firearm, Cesar claimed he was carrying a Rohm .38 revolver on the evening RFK was shot. He could have easily been carrying the same caliber revolver that he knew Sirhan would be equipped with. When interviewed by the LAPD, Cesar stated that he did draw his gun but never fired the weapon. He also claimed that he was knocked down after Sirhan's first shot and was unable to retaliate and fire his weapon. Cesar told investigators that he did own a .22-caliber Harrington & Richardson pistol and showed it to LAPD sergeant P.E. O'Steen on June 24, 1968. This conflicted with his original claim that he sold the gun to one Jim Yoder prior to the assassination. In October 1972, ex-FBI agent William Turner tracked down Yoder. Yoder showed Turner the receipt for the H&R pistol, dated September 6, 1968, contradicting Cesar's claim that he had sold the weapon months before the assassination.

The receipt included Cesar's signature. Nonetheless, the LAPD eliminated Cesar as a suspect without further interrogation. (d)

Cesar was considered a right-wing extremist who supported racist Alabama governor George Wallace and despised the Kennedy's. According to Lisa Pease, Cesar was part of a CIA assassination team formed to eliminate Robert Kennedy. She also discovered that from 1966-1970 he had worked for Hughes Aircraft, part of Howard Hughes' Organization. This was confirmed by John Meier, a top aide to Howard Hughes. On June 13, 1968, Meire wrote in his diary that Cesar's name was mentioned as one of the security guards on duty at the Ambassador Hotel on the evening of June 4, 1968. He wrote, "I remember Thane from his trips to Las Vegas where he was meeting with numerous gaming people and was introduced to me by Jack Hooper, an associate of Bob Maheu."

In an interview with Lisa Pease, John Meier told her that after hearing the radio broadcast, he "called someone and discussed the fact that I knew Thane Cesar who had been at the Ambassador that night." The next day, Meier was summoned by Maheu and severely admonished. "Maheu was furious and wanted to know why I was checking up on Thane. I was stunned at his anger, and he said to me that if I kept discussing this matter, he would see that I was no longer around the Hughes operation." Maheu did not want anyone to know that he personally knew Thane Cesar. The next day, Meier informed Pease, "Jack Hooper told me that he was speaking with Bob Maheu, and I was never to mention Thane Cesar's name or Bel Air Patrol." Bel Air Patrol was a California private security guard service owned by Maheu, where Cesar had worked prior to the assassination. Thane Cesar was working for Robert Maheu, a man with known connections to the Mafia and CIA. During

Pease's investigation she had discovered through two prominent online public records database aggregation services, that Cesar's profession was 'contract agent' for the CIA. This information would seem to confirm that Thane Cesar was in fact a CIA operative and more than likely assassinated Robert Kennedy upon orders given by Robert Maheu.

Richard Lubic, a television producer, was standing behind Robert Kennedy during the shooting. To his right, he noticed someone brandishing a gun but could not see who was holding it. When Kennedy fell to the ground, Lubic fell to the ground to help him and noticed a security guard, Thane Eugene Cesar, with his gun drawn, pointed towards the floor. Another eyewitness, Donald Schulman, claimed he saw Cesar fire his gun. Schulman also told the LAPD that he saw three separate guns in the pantry. Afterwards both men were intimidated in their homes by LAPD investigators, who also told Lubic, "don't bring this up, don't be talking about this" (additional shooters). Michael Wayne (perhaps spelled Wien) may have been an additional shooter.

On the evening of June 4, 1968, Wayne had gained access to the Kennedy suite on the fifth floor of the Ambassador Hotel. He followed the Kennedy entourage to the kitchen pantry and got RFK to sign some rolled-up posters before Kennedy gave his victory speech. (Eerily similar to Mark David Chapman with John Lennon at The Dakota building December, 8, 1980.)

RFK signs posters for Wayne. Note his appearance similar to Sirhan.

Wayne was asked to leave by security but returned into the crowd before the end of Kennedy's speech. After the speech, as RFK was being led through the pantry, Wayne followed, approximately ten feet behind Sirhan Sirhan. After the shooting, he ran from the scene but was taken into custody by a private guard named Agustus Mallard.

Wayne (L) in handcuffs by Mallard (R) shortly after RFK shooting.

After answering basic questions about his identity and what he had seen, Mallard released Wayne. On July 12, 1968, the LAPD brought Michael Wayne in for further questioning regarding a business card that was found amongst his possessions the night of June 4. The card belonged to Keith Duane Gilbert, a far-right conservative serving time in San Quentin prison for dynamite theft in 1965.

Sgt. Nielsen, who had been assigned to Foothill Detectives in 1966 was aware of Gilbert's background. He showed the copy of Gilbert's card to Lt. Manuel Pena, who was the commander of Foothill Detectives when Gilbert was being investigated regarding the stolen dynamite. Pena assigned Sgt. D.D. Varney to interview Michael Wayne to determine if there was any possible connection to Keith Gilbert. Wayne repeatedly denied knowing Gilbert. Nielsen then went to the Intelligence Division files and found both names, Michael Wayne and Keith Duane Gilbert cross-referenced.

Information provided to the LAPD indicated that Sirhan Sirhan, or a person who resembled him (Wayne?) was seen in an electrician's booth at the Ambassador Hotel at approximately 10:00 p.m. the night of the assassination. Wayne was interviewed again and released once more after answering a few basic questions.

The Special Unit Senator (SUS) investigation was trying to determine if a real estate scam from years ago could have any relevance to the RFK assassination. They had discovered that several LAPD officers were affiliated with the John Birch Society and also with another militant group, the Minutemen. They discovered that one officer in particular and Michael Wayne, had a definite connection to Keith Gilbert. In the spring of 1969, Wayne was brought in for questioning a third time.

Michael Wayne (Wien)

Sirhan Sirhan

On February 25, 1965, 1400 pounds of stolen dynamite was located in the garage apartment of Keith D. Gilbert, 419 Western, Glendale, California. The owner of this residence who lived in the main house was Mrs. Bernice Iverson, sister of LAPD Officer C.W. White. An Internal Affairs investigation into the dynamite burglary case resulted in White admitting he knew Dennis Mower, an acquaintance of Keith Gilbert. A background check of Gilbert was conducted to determine if he knew Officer White. When Gilbert was arrested, he was in possession of a business card with the inscription, 'Michael Wayne—Promoter." The two men's paths kept crossing.

On April 1, 1969, Gilbert was questioned in San Quentin prison by the LAPD regarding Wayne's business card and his connection with the Minutemen. Gilbert admitted to being a member of the Minutemen Society but denied knowing how he had received Wayne's business card. He intimated that he may have received the card from one of the many people he had met at a gun show in Yuma, Arizona, but denied knowing Wayne.

On the exact same day as Gilbert's interview, Lt. Enrique 'Hank' Hernandez called Michael Wayne in for yet another interview to determine why his card found at Gilbert's residence when Gilbert was arrested and how Gilbert's card was in Wayne's possession shortly after midnight, June 5, 1968, when he was questioned by the LAPD after the RFK shooting. At 1:00 p.m., April 10, 1968, Wayne was given a polygraph examination by Lt. Hernandez in room Poly-A at Parker Center. He passed the examination.

Sgt. Varney's initial report listed Wayne's behavior being more like a stalker than what he was, a hobbyist who collected signed political materials. Wayne routinely collected signed political items, so his asking RFK to sign a poster was not regarded as unusual. However, Varney determined that Wayne's entry into restricted access areas such as Kennedy's suite, and following RFK into the pantry before the victory speech, were questionable, especially since Wayne was asked to leave the pantry once he got the autograph but returned there before the end of Kennedy's speech. As a veteran law enforcement official, Varney expressed concern how easy it was for Wayne to walk right up to RFK and ask for an autograph; it went against his training as a police officer.

Varney also thought Wayne's resemblance to Sirhan may have been part of a misdirection strategy, using a Sirhan 'double' to cloud the water of any subsequent investigation. Wayne's connection to Intelligence had prepared him to answer questions from the LAPD and appear to be honest. However, it's entirely possible that he could have passed the polygraph examination while lying about his connections to Gilbert and his actions in the Ambassador. According to Lt. Hernandez, Wayne appeared not to have been involved, therefore making Sirhan Sirhan yet one more lone nut assassin, despite a plethora of evidence suggesting conspiracy, blanketed in a shroud of suspicion.

The authors support and affirm the idea (fact!) that Eugene Thane Cesar was clearly the individual who fatally wounded Senator Robert F. Kennedy. Admittedly, Sirhan Sirhan was there, and did in fact fire several shots at RFK. However, Cesar was clearly behind and at close range to the Senator, and the only one close enough to have delivered the killing blow as affirmed by Coroner Noguchi. We are mystified, saddened and angered that our Government has continued to promote the preposterous idea of Sirhan being the lone gunman, and the U.S. Media's deliberate and intentional support of this egregious lie.

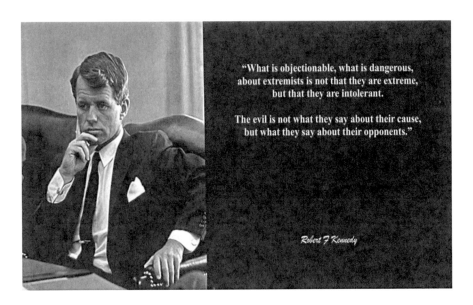

"What is objectionable, what is dangerous, about extremists is not that they are extreme, but that they are intolerant.

The evil is not what they say about their cause, but what they say about their opponents."

Robert F Kennedy

Eight

<u>LAPD and Media Complicity</u>

Despite numerous eyewitnesses who gave testimony that conflicted with the official report regarding RFK's death, the U.S. Media, under the influence of the LAPD and the CIA distorted eyewitness truth to promote their own heinous lies. This chapter will provide the facts and illustrate the cover-up perpetrated by these rogue agencies and the media.

Paul Schrade was the Western Regional Director of the United Auto Workers and a valuable confidant to Robert Kennedy and had introduced the Senator to Cesar Chavez and Dolores Huerta of the United Farm Workers. He was standing six feet behind Bobby as they entered the pantry. In 2018, Mr. Schrade told The Washington Post, "I was shaking violently, and I fell, then Bob fell. I saw flashes and heard crackling. The crackling actually was all the other bullets being fired." Other witnesses heard Senator Kennedy ask, "Is everybody OK? Is Paul all right?"

Among a hail of bullets, one struck Mr. Schrade's forehead. His skull had been fractured, but the bullet had not entered his brain. Several days after surgery to remove part of the bullet (some fragments remained), he met with reporters at Kaiser Foundation Hospital in Los Angeles. "I didn't see the gunman, there could have been one or ten." He actually believed there were two gunmen, Sirhan Sirhan, who shot him and four other people, and a different shooter who shot Senator Kennedy. On the 50th anniversary of the shooting, Schrade told The Washington Post that the LAPD failed do their best to find the second gunman, and that more than eight bullets from Sirhan's .22 caliber revolver had been fired in the pantry. "Yes, he (Sirhan) did shoot me. Yes, he shot four other people and aimed at Kennedy. The important thing is he did not shoot Robert Kennedy. Why didn't they go after the second gunman?" (a)

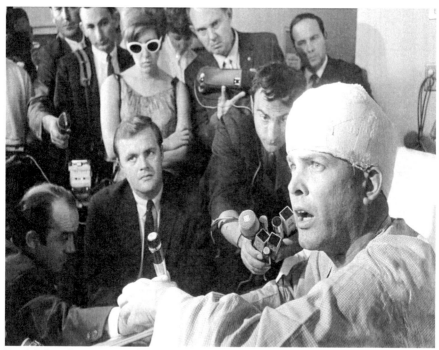

Paul Schrade meets with reporters June 10, 1968, Kaiser Hospital.

It was Schrade's lifelong belief that Sirhan did not kill Senator Kennedy, and this led him to attend Sirhan's 15th parole hearing in 2016, where he apologized to Sirhan for not attending previous hearings and not fighting harder for Sirhan's release. He was quoted by the Associated Press at the hearing as stating, "I should have been here long ago, and that's why I feel guilty for not being here to help you and to help me." As Sirhan Sirhan left the hearing, Schrade said, "I'm sorry this is happening to you, this is my fault!" Clearly this was not Paul Schrade's fault.

However, he was consumed with guilt, knowing for 50 years that the autopsy report and his own investigation clearly showed Sirhan Sirhan was innocent of killing Robert Kennedy. In 2021, Schrade recorded a video supporting Sirhan's upcoming bid for parole. In the video he stated, "I don't excuse him for what he did, but I don't excuse the LAPD and the District Attorney's office for 52 years of saying he's guilty when he is not." Senator Kennedy's son, Douglas, attended the virtual hearing and urged for his release as well. Robert Kennedy, Jr. wrote a letter (see Ambassador Hotel Chapter) supporting Sirhan's release. Although the parole board recommended Sirhan's release, California Governor Gavin Newsom later reversed the decision and denied his parole once again. Newsom said to the Los Angeles Times, "Mr. Sirhan's assassination of Senator Kennedy is among the most notorious crimes in American history. After decades in prison, he has failed to address the deficiencies that led him to assassinate Senator Kennedy. Mr. Sirhan lacks the insight that would prevent him from making the same types of dangerous decisions he made in the past." (b) When asked about possible CIA involvement, Schrade said, "It's possible...I mean, they've done worse things haven't they?" (c)

Daryl Gates

Daryl Gates joined the LAPD on September 16, 1949. As an officer, he was hand-picked to be the chauffeur for Chief William Parker. Gates often stated that he gained administrative and professional insights from Parker during the many hours they spent together each day. He may also have learned how to cover-up and frame crimes. When he was promoted to lieutenant, Gates became Parker's executive officer. He would continue to get promoted during his career, and became an inspector responsible for intelligence, and was instrumental in the Watts riots in 1965 and the Manson Family murders. In 1975, he was Assistant Chief of the LAPD and was deeply involved in the special investigation into the assassination of Robert F. Kennedy.

According to an article in the LA Free Press, the LAPD and Daryl Gates were negligent in misplacing and/or destroying evidence critical to the investigation regarding RFK's murder. In mid-August 1975, the second gunman theory was gaining momentum from the Los Angeles County Board of Supervisors and the Los Angeles City Council. Councilor Zev Yaroslavsky asked the LAPD to make available all evidence related to JFK's assassination in their possession. This request led to the City Attorney's office and the LAPD sheepishly admitting that much of the requested material was simply not available. On August 21 at a meeting of the Police Commission, President Samuel Williams and LAPD Asst. Chief Daryl Gates gave an accounting of what the police department had and did not have.

Specific reference was made to the motion introduced by Yaroslavsky and seconded by eight other councilors. That motion set forth crucial areas of evidence which unofficial assassination investigators have claimed might provide proof as to whether a second gun was fired in the pantry of the Ambassador Hotel. Listed here is the police account of the disposition of the items requested by the LA City Council.

Statements of Eyewitnesses to the Shooting.

All of these statements are available to be reviewed on a court order of the presiding judge in Los Angeles Superior Court. The only statements listed were those marked as identification, some which were used in the Sirhan Sirhan trial. Conspiracy theorists and others have maintained that some of the eyewitness statements conflict with the police version of the shooting.

The 10-Volume Summary of the Police Investigation.

In August 1975, there were currently three copies of these summaries. Two were with the LAPD 'under lock and key,' and one was being held by the FBI.

The Doorjamb.

The bullet holes in a doorjamb and in ceiling panels would account for more bullet holes than Sirhan had bullets in his gun, along with the five other victims besides Robert Kennedy, but both were destroyed, at the direction of an order issued on June 27, 1969 by members of the LAPD. This was merely nine weeks after Sirhan was found guilty. According to Daryl Gates, "the primary reason they were not kept was they had no useful purpose. They had been investigated at the time of the investigation." This was equivalent to LBJ ordering the Presidential Limousine completely restored before Oswald ever went to trial. If there were bullet holes in the doorjamb, it would help prove conspiracy, that more than eight bullets were fired from Sirhan's gun. There is no way Sirhan could have re-loaded and fired an additional 4-6 shots before being subdued.

Tests Proved Nothing.

"It was the conclusion of the criminalist at the scene in his detailed examination that it was not a bullet hole, but because of the intensiveness of the investigation, they (LAPD) decided to take the doorjamb and make further tests. These tests proved absolutely nothing and so the doorjamb was, through our normal and regular procedures disposed of," said Gates. This explanation is ridiculous. How many times have appeals courts overthrown testimony and asked to see the original evidence? Destroyed by regular procedures? This was an investigation into the assassination of a sitting Senator of the United States who was running for President.

The Ceiling Panels and the X-Rays of the Panels.

The ceiling panels were also destroyed pursuant to the same order which removed the doorjamb. Commission President Williams pointed out that the order came after Sirhan's trial and sentencing. He stated, "we are informed that some X-rays of the ceiling panel were taken, but we have been unable to locate the X-rays." Gates chimed in to say that normally the panels would not have been removed. Their value as evidence, he amplified, was "while they were in place. From their position we could determine the trajectory; we could determine the number of shots, the number of bullet holes, all of those kinds of things, and they were examined while they were in place, and photographs were taken so that all the needed evidence was gathered at that time." If Gates was suggesting that the value of the evidence was only necessary while in its original position in the pantry, why were they removed, examined, and x-rayed in the first place? Gates continued to say, "we took the ceiling panels simply because of the intensiveness of the investigation. They were examined in the laboratory, they were X-rayed. Nothing new was found that we didn't already know. They were absolutely no value for evidence and so they were again destroyed under normal procedures. This was at the end of the investigation when we (LAPD) were putting together the files and culling out the useless material." Gates then explained that normal disposal procedure calls for destroying material for which is determined to be of no further use after the case in question has been adjudicated. He said, "If we didn't do that, I'm quite certain we'd need another building as large as the Parker Center to house all of that useless material." Useless material? This was evidence of a crime. Why after nearly 100 years is the car Bonnie and Clyde were killed in displayed in a Casino on the border of Nevada and California? Why is John Wilkes Booth's pistol on display at Ford's

Theater? There are thousands of artifacts used in criminal trials, preserved for future researchers and on display for the general public. It is part of our history as the United States. Why was Daryl Gates destroying crucial evidence immediately after Sirhan's trial?

The Left Sleeve of Senator Kennedy's Jacket.

"That sleeve is not available," said Commission President Williams. Why wasn't it available? Wasn't Senator Kennedy's clothing cut off of him at one of the two hospitals where he received medical treatment? Had the sleeve been made available, it may have revealed powder burns, placing an assassin closer to Kennedy than where Sirhan was standing. Gates explained that the sleeve had never been available to the police department. He said, "one of the doctors attending Kennedy recalls doing some cutting on the coat." Gates was suggesting that the Doctor may have removed the left sleeve from RFK's coat. All of the police photographs of the jacket show the left sleeve missing. As someone who has worked in an emergency room, (author Fannin) it is standard operating procedure to place all personal belongings and valuables taken from a body and place them in a sealed and documented container for the family or police (if a crime has occurred) to have. The missing sleeve was noted in court testimony. Sirhan's defense attorneys were not concerned with the number of bullets allegedly fired at Senator Kennedy, nor were they concerned with material evidence. They were simply trying to prevent Sirhan Sirhan from being sentenced to death. Dion Morrow, an assistant city attorney, explained that the Senator's clothing passed through several hands before it got to the LAPD, including those of a doctor, two nurses, Ethel Kennedy, and a priest. Of note, the family would not have the rights to any personal artifacts since a crime had occurred. The clothing should have immediately been placed into evidence by the LAPD. Explaining the evidence away after the fact does not excuse the LAPD of negligence in their duties.

The Reenactment Films of the Shooting of Kennedy.

In November 1968, the District Attorney's office made reenactment films depicting the assassination, using the witnesses present at the time. As of 1975, the District Attorney's office has a copy of the film as does CBS News. The LAPD does not possess a copy. Karl Uecker, a participant in the film and a witness to the shooting, is reported to have claimed the film was a 'phony.' Uecker says the police attempted to prove their 'lone gunman theory' through careful direction of the film.

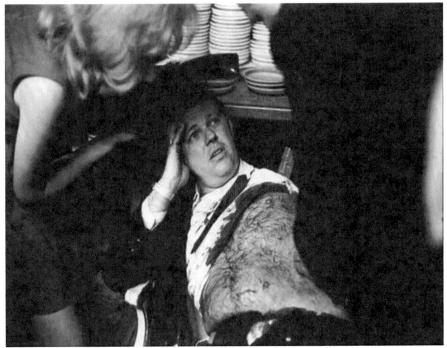

Image of reenactment film made by the L.A. District Attorney's office.

The Spectrographic Analysis of Bullets & Fragments.

Through their tests, Ballistics experts have determined that two different types of bullets which could not have come from the same gun were fired in the pantry that evening. Unless these experts were grossly incorrect in their conclusions, this point alone confirms a conspiracy. Describing their actions Gates said, "the criminalist did inform us that he did make a spectrographic analysis." He continued, "again that under the circumstances he would not ordinarily have made one because he did not believe that it would prove or disprove anything, but again it was an intensive investigation, and he wanted to make sure that he had covered every possibility." After examination of the spectrographic analysis, Gates concluded "that it provided nothing to him. Nothing that he didn't already know and that was placed in the file and again, through the ordinary disposal procedures, that spectrographic analysis was destroyed."

Still Photographs.

According to Commission President Williams, there were literally hundreds of photos taken at the scene and of Senator Kennedy. Many of the photographs were entered into evidence in Sirhan's trial, he said, and added, "the department is in possession of pictures not used at that trial. We are not reluctant to make those photographs available." Dion Morrow admitted that his office would not be willing to release autopsy photographs of Robert Kennedy's body. The Police Commission agreed to establish a procedure permitting release of certain materials collected in the assassination investigation. They appointed a five-member committee consisting of Commissioner Mariana Pfaelzer, Gates, two investigators and a member of the City Attorney's office to review written requests for physical evidence or files. They would deliver the answers in writing but could also ask to meet with 'individuals or entities' requesting follow-up material. Doesn't this sound suspiciously similar to Allen Dulles, former Director of the CIA, being appointed to the Warren Commission to investigate JFK's death? Gates could simply squash any witness or testimony which could damage LAPD credibility. The Committee emphasized it would not release material which might invade the privacy of third parties. Pfaelzer explained, "the files do contain embarrassing details of people's lives." She didn't elaborate further. During a council hearing to ascertain the disposition of evidence said to be missing, Yaroslavsky commented, "One would have thought that our authorities would have been a little more sensitive to destruction of evidence in this particular case than they would have in a normal homicide in the city of Los Angeles. This was not a normal homicide. This was an assassination of a United States Senator...it was an assassination and a homicide that had its ramifications not only in this community, but through the country and the world, and we lost the evidence."

A colleague on the Committee, Robert Farrell, offered a different perspective of the attention focused on reopening the investigation of the Kennedy assassination. He said, "I think it's important that when it's Senator Kennedy that's dead that we do these extraordinary things, but a lot of people die in my community by police gunfire." He continued, "and let me tell you, if you open it up here for Bobby Kennedy, be prepared to open it up for guys in South Los Angeles and members of this Committee, you have never done that. Bobby Kennedy has gone and it's over. What about the people who, we feel—some of us in the community—may be getting shot down today? If people want to know, and they know the police have the information, if it's going to be the policy...to open it up for situations that involve the great, make sure we open it up in such a way that it's available to the people by comparison may be small in stature, but they're human beings too." (d) Farrell was clearly stating that if the LAPD and this Committee to investigate were contemplating these actions with Robert Kennedy, what was to stop a third-rate burglary victim from receiving the same attention. Again, Daryl Gates would never condone such nonsense.

Another article was released through UPI on April 22, 1988. It was titled, 'Key RFK Photo, report withheld by police.'

SACRAMENTO, Calif.—A key photograph taken during the investigation of Robert F. Kennedy's 1968 assassination was kept secret by Los Angeles police who feared it might contradict official statement, newly released files show. In a revelation one expert called 'astounding,' the documents show police attempted to answer specific questions about the killing raised by Rep. Allard Lowenstein (D-NY) 14 years ago (1974) but withheld the answers from the public until the files were opened at the state archives in Sacramento this week.

A lengthy internal memo in December 1974 from detectives to Assistant Chief Daryl Gates, responds point-by-point to questions about the case posed in a letter by former Rep. Allard Lowenstein, (D-NY) a one-time Kennedy associate. The answers generally restate the official police accounts that Palestinian immigrant Sirhan Bishara Sirhan acted alone when he shot Kennedy June 5, 1968, in the pantry of the Ambassador Hotel in Los Angeles. One notable exception, however, is contained in a separate 'confidential addendum to the Lowenstein inquiry.'

Allard K. Lowenstein

The addendum indicates there existed a photograph that compared a bullet removed from Kennedy's body to a bullet from a test-firing of Sirhan's gun, but that was not introduced as evidence in Sirhan's 1969 trial. The photo later was deliberately kept secret as potentially harmful to then Police Chief Ed Davis and other officials. A poor reproduction of the picture was attached to the memo, but the actual photo has not been located yet in the archives.

While the photograph is said to support the police version that Sirhan fired the fatal shots and 'should be effective rebuttal evidence were this case ever to be retried,' the 1974 memo also says that the photo's existence could have contradicted Davis's public statements. 'The information has not been revealed prior to this report and may conflict with previous statements made by the chief of police and other officials,' the memo said. 'The existence of this photograph is believed to be unknown by anyone outside of this department,' the memo continues. 'The release of this information at this time would be susceptible to criticism because lay people would in all probability have difficulty deciphering the photograph. The issue as to its not being revealed at an earlier time may further make its authenticity suspect, particularly to the avid, exact assassination buff.'

The memo responding to Lowenstein's questions, and the secret addendum, had not been made public or revealed to Lowenstein, according to Gregory Stone, a political scientist and Kennedy assassination expert. Lowenstein was one of the first public figures to cast doubt upon the official account of the assassination of Senator Robert Kennedy. He made a one-hour appearance on the PBS television show, 'Firing Line' in 1975, hosted by William F. Buckley Jr., in which he stated that he did not believe that Sirhan Sirhan alone had shot Kennedy. In fact, Lowenstein said, "Robert Kennedy's death, like the President's, was mourned as an extension of senseless violence; events moved on, and the profound alterations that these deaths...brought in the equation of power in America was perceived as random. What is odd is not that some people thought it was all random, but that so many intelligent people refused to believe that it might be anything else. Nothing can measure more graphically how limited was the general understanding of what is possible in America."

On March 14, 1980, Lowenstein was shot and killed in his Manhattan office by Dennis Sweeney, who was mentally ill and believed that Lowenstein was plotting against him. Sweeney then calmly waited for the police to arrive. Sweeney was later found not guilty by reason of insanity. At Lowenstein's funeral in New York City on March 18, 1980, eulogies were delivered by William

F. Buckley, Jr., and Senator Edward M. Kennedy. Lowenstein is buried in Arlington National Cemetery approximately 100' west of President John F. Kennedy.

"I'm very surprised, I didn't know there were replies to Lowenstein's questions," said Stone when showed the memo. He continued, "That's astounding." A LAPD spokesman had no immediate comment on the memo.

Former Chief Davis, said he did not remember the secret photo, but that it probably didn't contain important evidence. "If it has some evidentiary value, regardless of who it impacted, it should have been released," he said, "But the evidentiary value is determined by the trial, and the trial had long since been held."

Researchers were quick to point out, however, that physical evidence from the crime scene never came under close examination at the trial because Sirhan admitted to shooting Kennedy and the defense focused on his state of mind.

Stone speculated that in 1974, police decided to keep the existence of the photograph secret, fearing it would fuel speculation they were withholding critical evidence in the case. "I'd say that's a pretty devastating piece of evidence," said Dan Moldea, an author and investigative journalist who has studied the Kennedy killing. During a telephone interview he said the memo supports charges police 'obstructed independent attempts to resolve critical issues in the case.'

The LAPD officially closed their investigation in July 1969, and resisted pressure to open their voluminous files until 1987, when they reached an agreement to turn over most of the material to the state. When the 50,000 documents, 2,900 photos and other evidence were put on display for the first time, it was revealed police inexplicably burned 2,410 photos that had been gathered in the case two months after the shooting.

Nearly 40 years after Robert Kennedy's assassination, the U.S. Media continues to parrot obvious falsehoods. On the surface, the June 2007 documentary titled, 'Conspiracy Test—The RFK Assassination,' by the Discovery and National Geographic (together known as Discovery Times Channel) television networks appears to validate conspiracy in the RFK's assassination. Both networks interviewed Mel Ayton, author of 'The Forgotten Terrorist—Sirhan Sirhan and the Murder of Senator Robert F. Kennedy.' (f)

The documentary challenged the 'Pruszynski Tape.' This tape contained the original audio recordings of RFK finishing his victory speech, including up to and after the shots were fired in the Ambassador Hotel pantry. The recording was made by Stanislaw Pruszynski, a journalist covering RFK's campaign in Los Angeles. In the documentary they use research compiled from two teams of experts, Philip Harrison and Professor Peter French of J P French Associates in the United Kingdom and Steve Barber, Dr. Chad Zimmerman and Michael O'Dell in the United States.

J P French Associates is the United Kingdom's oldest established independent forensic speech and acoustics laboratory. The company prepares reports for the defense and prosecution in criminal cases on speaker identification, transcription, authentication and enhancement of recordings, acoustic investigation, and other related areas, including the analysis of recorded gun shots, and is regularly involved in some of the most important and high-profile cases in the United Kingdom and around the world.

Philip Harrison is considered an expert on audio recordings. During his analysis of the Pruszynski Tape, he used three different methods:

1) Listening analytically to the recording via headphones.
2) Examining visual representations of the recording's waveform, and
3) Analyzing plots of sound energy across frequency over time, all using specialized computer software.

Harrison and Professor French found no more than 8 shots were present on the recording. However, if they only found 8 shots, how do they explain four shots (three hitting RFK) and five other victims with one shot each, for a total of 9 shots. Even if they still rely upon the acoustic evidence, it obviously doesn't match the ballistic evidence. The UK and US teams independently examined the tape and then Barber and Harrison consulted together.

The Discovery Times Channel documentary acoustics research was led by Philip Van Praag, an electrical engineer, and author of 'Evolution of the Audio Recorder.' Wes Dooley, forensic analyst and manufacturer of ribbon microphones was brought in to independently study the recording. Van Praag claimed that he had identified approximately 13 shot sounds on the Pruszynski Tape, whilst Dooley and his team located 10. Van Praag also stated, "there were certainly more than 8 shots fired." Author Dan Moldea, who wrote his own book on the RFK assassination, 'The Killing of Robert F. Kennedy: An Investigation of Motive, Means, and Opportunity,' after watching the documentary said, "Van Praag has concluded—and stated on national television— that thirteen shots were fired at the crime scene. Even the kookiest kook hasn't suggested that." If Moldea was capable of simple math, (four shots at RFK, five other individuals with wounds and evidence of five bullet holes in the pantry doorjambs and ceiling tile) he would never have concluded that only eight shots were fired. The injuries to Paul Schrade and Elizabeth Evans were in the forehead and did not pass through their bodies. William Weisel was shot in the abdomen and this bullet never exited his body. The only two injured victims where the bullets could have possibly exited were Ira Goldstein (left hip) and Irwin Stroll (left lower leg). Thus, if those two bullets passed through Goldstein and Stroll and went on to strike the doorjamb, there would only have been two holes instead of four. Yet one more bullet was lodged in the ceiling tile. Assuming four bullets were fired at RFK, five other victims were wounded with two of those lodging in the doorjamb, two additional bullets also in the doorjamb and one lodged in the ceiling, a minimum of twelve shots were fired. This is only one shot less than the thirteen that Van Praag claims to hear on the tape. And we are taking a leap of faith that both bullets that injured Goldstein and Stroll continued on to cause damage to the doorjamb. For Dan Moldea to say that Van Praag 'is the kookiest kook,' we have to assume he cannot comprehend simple mathematics.

In the May-June 1998 issue of Probe, the official newsletter of the Citizens for Truth about the Kennedy Assassination (CTKA), Jim DiEugenio accuses Dan Moldea of being a CIA contract agent. Naturally, Moldea vehemently denied the allegation. He claimed to be a target of CTKA's active disinformation campaign. However, his Wikipedia page lists him as a non-fiction author.

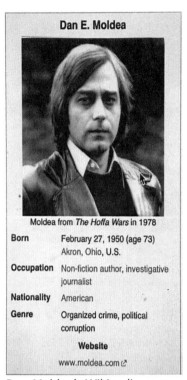

Dan E. Moldea

Moldea from *The Hoffa Wars* in 1978

Born	February 27, 1950 (age 73) Akron, Ohio, U.S.
Occupation	Non-fiction author, investigative journalist
Nationality	American
Genre	Organized crime, political corruption

Website

www.moldea.com ⬈

Dan Moldea's Wikipedia page.

Does this mean his book is his version of events or is it actually based on the crime? Moldea said of the Discovery Times Channel documentary, "I thought that this program was very exciting and well done, just as I thought that Oliver Stone's 'JFK' was very exciting and well done. The problem is that both presentations defy belief. In other words, good dramas, terrible history." Interestingly enough, Moldea, of his own accord, admits to interviewing Thane Cesar dozens of times. Moreover, Cesar passed a lie-detector test that Moldea had arranged. Isn't it convenient that Cesar would meet with a non-fiction writer dozens of times at no cost, yet when confronted with an interview with Robert Kennedy Jr. abruptly asked for $25,000 for the interview?

Although Moldea denies being on the CIA payroll his actions and book reviews suggest otherwise, just like researcher and former Curator of the Sixth Floor Museum in Dealey Plaza, Gary Mack. Mack was a strong conspiracy theorist who participated in Nigel Turner's 'The Men Who Killed Kennedy' documentary series in 1988. However, immediately after becoming curator of the museum, his opinions quickly reverted to non-conspiracy. Robert Groden, who released the Zapruder Film on national television on Geraldo Rivera's 'Late Night America' program said, "the biggest thing about Gary (Mack) taking the job at the Book Depository building is that I lost a good friend." He continued, "He could no longer speak the truth about the JFK assassination."

Mack's 180 on conspiracy were much like those of former FOX News host Bill O'Reilly, who pulled his own incredible switcheroo in order to parrot anything the network wanted him to say and has been known to fabricate the truth if it might help his ratings. While at 'Inside Edition' and WFAA-TV in Dallas, O'Reilly was a strong advocate of conspiracy theories. When he moved on to FOX News and wrote his fictional tome, 'Killing Kennedy,' he suddenly and inexplicably now professed to believe that Oswald alone was guilty of killing JFK. Moldea, Mack and O'Reilly all realized that in today's media, lies pay better than the truth. If you write a book stating that Lee Oswald or Sirhan Sirhan are guilty and lone assassins, you get rave reviews from The New York Times, The Washington Post, and etc. Gerald Posner's 1993 hysterically false and completely fabricated book 'Case Closed' has a 4.5 out of 5-star rating (nearly 1000 reviews) and was later proven to be replete with plagiarism and lies. Robert Groden's (Among the first and most important researchers into JFK's murder) book, 'High Treason' was mentioned in a Washington

Post column titled, 'Historians, Buffs and Crackpots.' (g) High Treason has several versions now available on Amazon but has less than 100 reviews. Groden has always believed in conspiracy in the JFK assassination and has written several compelling books based on irrefutable research. He was offered the Curator position at the Sixth Floor Museum in Dealey Plaza with an annual salary of over $225,000 in 1990 and refused the position. He stated, "they (6th Floor Museum) specifically told me if I took the position, I could not discuss conspiracy." Mack, the original Curator died in 2015. The current Curator also cannot discuss or sell any conspiracy related books in the museum's gift shop. Moldea's fictional RFK book is available there.

CNN reporter Brad Johnson also studied the Pruszynski Tape and claims the evidence proves more than eight shots were fired in the pantry of the Ambassador Hotel. He told Moldea in 2005, "After having listened to this recording many times over a number of months, I believe that I am hearing 10 shots as follows: two shots fired in quick succession and then a string of eight shots fired in quick succession. An acoustics expert here in Atlanta has just issued a confidential report on this recording that concludes there are nine high-probability gunshots captured in this tape. One less than what I believe I'm hearing, but one more than Sirhan Sirhan could have fired."

Johnson had matched the Pruszynski Tape to CBS footage and counted eleven shots. Below is the timeline he provided to Moldea:

12:16:00.5 am PDT - The first shot or shots are fired in the kitchen pantry (to my hearing, there are two shots being fired in quick succession at this time but presently an examination of my acoustics expert can confirm the high probability of only one shot).

12:16:01.0 am PDT - A mysterious "thump" sound is heard but at this point in my research it appears unlikely this sound was a gunshot.

12:16:04.0 am PDT - By this time, a string of eight additional shots have been fired (all eight are high probability shots according to my acoustics expert). Our count of high-probability gunshots is now 9.

12:16:05.0 am PDT - A long, very high-pitched female scream is heard in the kitchen pantry.

12:16:18.5 am PDT - Andy West turns his tape recorder back on, upon entering the kitchen pantry (his recorder has been off for the past 66.5 seconds).

12:16:55.0 am PDT - Two more high probability shots are fired as a struggle with Sirhan Sirhan continues for his handgun (since Sirhan emptied his weapon, these could have been the last two bullets discharged as a result of the struggle). Our count of high-probability gunshots is now 11.

12:17:41.0 am PDT - Andy West shouts into his microphone, "Ladies and gentlemen, they have the gun away from the man."

CNN would then make the following preposterous statement, "This new acoustics evidence in the RFK case suggests to a high degree of probability that on the night of June 4/5, 1968 in the Ambassador Hotel pantry there were no other gunmen who fired shots at Senator Kennedy. Furthermore, this evidence negates to a high degree of probability the allegation by conspiracy advocates that extra bullets were either discovered or retrieved from the pantry's swinging doors." Apparently both CNN and Moldea are incapable of comprehending simple mathematics.

Robert Kennedy, like his brother John, was a great danger to those virulent forces of war and oppression within his own government, and he died as a true patriot for opposing them. If we wish to honor him, we are obligated to pursue the truth as to why he died and why it still matters. No government agency will ever do that for us. Fifty-five years of silence must be ended, and it is up to us to keep searching for the truth. RFK, like his brother John, was assassinated by a CIA-run operation intended to silence their voices of courageous resistance to an expanding secret government dedicated to war, murder, and human exploitation, the U.S. government of today. The murders of JFK, Malcolm X, MLK, and RFK may never be brought to justice because they are deeply ingrained within the institutional structure of the U.S. Government and CIA-controlled major American media.

"What we need in the United States is not division,
what we need in the United States is not hatred,
what we need in the United States
is not violence or lawlessness,
but love and wisdom,
and compassion toward one another
and a feeling of justice toward
those who still suffer within our country,
whether they be white or they be black."

Robert F. Kennedy

Nine

<u>How Many Cooks Were in the Kitchen?</u>

This chapter is a brief summary of all the people in the pantry when Robert Kennedy was shot and statements or viewpoints provided by some of these individuals.

Senator Robert Kennedy—Fatal victim of shooting.

Ethel Kennedy—Wife of Senator Kennedy.

Paul Schrade—United Auto Workers Union and Kennedy's campaign labor chair. The most vocal of all critics of the assassination of Robert Kennedy and a victim of shooting.

Ira Goldstein—A 19-year-old radio reporter for Continental News Service and victim of shooting.

William Weisel—Associate news director for ABC News and victim of shooting.

Irwin Stroll—A 17-year-old campaign volunteer and victim of shooting.

Elizabeth Evans—A Democratic activist and victim of shooting.

Pete Hamill—Writer who has written for numerous national magazines, has worked as a syndicated columnist, and was most recently Editor in chief of the New York Daily News. Hamill sent letter to RFK encouraging him to run for President.

Rosy Grier—Security for Senator Kennedy. He was instrumental in grabbing Sirhan's gun/wrist immediately after the initial shots were fired.

George Plimpton—He was an actor and writer, known for appearances in Good Will Hunting (1997), Nixon (1995) and Just Cause (1995). Close friend of Robert Kennedy who helped subdue Sirhan.

Freddy Plimpton—Wife of George Plimpton (1968-1988).

Rafer Johnson—Security for Senator Kennedy. With Grier and Plimpton helped subdue Sirhan.

William Barry—FBI agent who placed his jacket under Bobby's head and later discovered additional bullet holes in doorframe of Ambassador kitchen.

Sirhan Sirhan—Accused and convicted assassin.

Thane Eugene Cesar—Suspected assassin.

Michael Wayne—Bookstore clerk, possible accomplice.

Vincent DiPierro—eyewitness (waiter) to shooting, standing near RFK.

Karl Uecker—eyewitness to shooting, standing near RFK.

Boris Yaro—eyewitness/photographer to shooting, standing near RFK.

Juan Romero—eyewitness to shooting near RFK, was photographed with Kennedy after the assassination.

Sandra Serrano—Witness, told police that a girl in a polka dot dress first entered the Embassy Room via a fire escape, accompanied by two men. According to Serrano the girl fled with one of her accomplices down the same fire escape about 20 minutes after they had arrived, proclaiming "We shot Kennedy." as they left. Serrano was interrogated by the LAPD who tried to get her to recant her story. To her credit, she has always maintained the girl in the polka dot dress was involved in the shooting.

Geraldine Agnes McCarthy—Shortly after midnight on June 5, 1968, she and several members of her family left the stage and went to a small alcove to the left of the stage and near the rear of the ballroom. This alcove had access to a stairway leading up to the Embassy Room and also had access to an outside door opening onto the Wilshire Street parking lot of the hotel. She stated that immediately outside this doorway to the parking lot there was a fire escape leading down from the floor above.

Margaret McCarthy—with members of her family were in this alcove attempting to get a breath of fresh air when several people came down the stairway from above and a girl in an orange dress stated, "Kennedy has been shot." Shortly after that a girl in a 'beige dress with black dots' came down the outside fire escape and exclaimed, "Oh my God, Kennedy's been shot."

Winnie Marshall—witness with McCarthy family.

Mary Towley—witness with McCarthy family.

Eileen Anderson—witness with McCarthy family.

Phil Litroh—witness with McCarthy family.

Chris Marshall—witness with McCarthy family.

Paul Benedict—witness with McCarthy family.

Albert Victor Ellis—He heard a female voice state "We shot him." He assumed at the time this person meant we the people. He then left the Embassy Room and went out into the lobby.

John Shamel—Ambassador Hotel's Convention Manager.

Richard Lubic—a television producer, was standing behind Robert Kennedy during the shooting. He saw someone holding a gun but could not see the shooter. After Kennedy fell to the ground, Lubic fell to the ground to help him and saw a security guard, Thane Eugene Cesar, with his gun drawn and pointed towards the floor.

Laurie Gail Porter—was in the Embassy Room during RFK's victory speech. After hearing the shots from about 50 feet away she heard her friend Robin Casden shout, "We shot him". She did recall…there were several people who shouted, "We shot him" and she attributed the exclamation to the hysterical nature of the situation.

Robin Casden—Friend of Laurie Porter.

Mr. and Mrs. Bernstein—shortly after the shooting told LAPD Sergeant Paul Sharaga, they had observed a young woman in a polka dot dress, accompanied by a young man, laughing and shouting "We shot him."

Valerie Schulte—Possible suspect as polka dot girl.

Howard 'Cap' Hardy—saw a young woman in the pantry at the time of the shooting and she had been wearing a "…sleeveless dress, off-white in color, with navy blue circles on it. The blue circles were of different sizes and the smaller circles had a white peace symbol in them and the larger circles had the word 'McCarthy' in lower case white letters."

Darnell Johnson—stated he saw a woman in a polka dot dress near Kennedy and that she fled the scene with a man after the shooting.

George Green—stated that the polka dot girl and her accomplice/accomplices were the only people attempting to leave the pantry at the time of the shooting or immediately afterwards.

Security Guard Jack Merritt—Believes Green was mistaken in his belief that the polka dot girl and her accomplices were the only people fleeing the pantry at the time of the shooting. "In the confusion [Merritt] noticed, among others, two men and a woman leave the kitchen through a back exit....she was wearing a polka dot dress....other people also left."

Charles D. White—fled the pantry at the time of the shooting or shortly after the shots had been fired.

Thomas Perez—fled the pantry at the time of the shooting or shortly after the shots had been fired.

Uno Timanson—fled the pantry at the time of the shooting or shortly after the shots had been fired.

Angelo DiPierro—fled the pantry at the time of the shooting or shortly after the shots had been fired.

Robin Karen Casden—fled the pantry at the time of the shooting or shortly after the shots had been fired.

Barbara Rubin—fled the pantry at the time of the shooting or shortly after the shots had been fired.

James W. Lowe—fled the pantry at the time of the shooting or shortly after the shots had been fired.

Gonzalo Cetina-Carrillo—fled the pantry at the time of the shooting or shortly after the shots had been fired.

Trudy Jennings—fled the pantry at the time of the shooting or shortly after the shots had been fired.

Richard D. Little—recalled "...one of the Kennedy girls ...came running out of the kitchen to the lobby of the Embassy Room shouting, they shot him."

Fred Meenedsen—saw a "...man calling for a doctor (who) came running out. Next, an unknown woman...ran through these kitchen doors and said Kennedy had been shot as she went towards the lobby."

Harry Benson—said that after the shooting he "...went outside the ballroom where there was a white male....with a United States flag in his mouth....a real nutty guy who said something such as Thank God, he's been shot."

Henrietta Sterlitz—saw "...two teenage boys and one teenage girl ...pop balloons and... exclaim 'Kennedy's Dead!"

Evelyn Planavsk—saw "...two teenage boys and one teenage girl ...pop balloons and... exclaim 'Kennedy's Dead!"

Nina Rhodes—In 1992 Rhodes told conspiracy authors that she heard anywhere from 10-14 shots.

Harold Edward Hughes—claimed only 8 shots were fired despite the physical evidence of at least 9, four in Robert Kennedy and one each in five other victims.

Ralph Elmore—claimed only 8 shots were fired despite the physical evidence of at least 9, four in Robert Kennedy and one each in five other victims.

Jesse Unruh—claimed only 8 shots were fired despite the physical evidence of at least 9, four in Robert Kennedy and one each in five other victims.

Estelyn LaHive—claimed only 8 shots were fired despite the physical evidence of at least 9, four in Robert Kennedy and one each in five other victims.

Joseph A. LaHive—claimed only 8 shots were fired despite the physical evidence of at least 9, four in Robert Kennedy and one each in five other victims.

Richard Aubry—claimed only 8 shots were fired despite the physical evidence of at least 9, four in Robert Kennedy and one each in five other victims.

David Saul Barrett—claimed only 8 shots were fired despite the physical evidence of at least 9, four in Robert Kennedy and one each in five other victims.

Richard L. Cohen—claimed only 8 shots were fired despite the physical evidence of at least 9, four in Robert Kennedy and one each in five other victims.

David M. Esquith—claimed only 8 shots were fired despite the physical evidence of at least 9, four in Robert Kennedy and one each in five other victims.

Jacqueline Sullivan—claimed only 8 shots were fired despite the physical evidence of at least 9, four in Robert Kennedy and one each in five other victims.

James Cummings—claimed only 8 shots were fired despite the physical evidence of at least 9, four in Robert Kennedy and one each in five other victims.

Paul Green Houston—claimed only 8 shots were fired despite the physical evidence of at least 9, four in Robert Kennedy and one each in five other victims.

Richard Edward Drew—claimed only 8 shots were fired despite the physical evidence of at least 9, four in Robert Kennedy and one each in five other victims.

Bob Funk—claimed only 8 shots were fired despite the physical evidence of at least 9, four in Robert Kennedy and one each in five other victims.

Robert Anthony Toigo—claimed only 8 shots were fired despite the physical evidence of at least 9, four in Robert Kennedy and one each in five other victims.

Barbara Rubin—claimed only 8 shots were fired despite the physical evidence of at least 9, four in Robert Kennedy and one each in five other victims.

Lon Bruce Rubin—claimed only 8 shots were fired despite the physical evidence of at least 9, four in Robert Kennedy and one each in five other victims.

Dun Gifford—claimed only 8 shots were fired despite the physical evidence of at least 9, four in Robert Kennedy and one each in five other victims.

Charles Bailey—claimed only 8 shots were fired despite the physical evidence of at least 9, four in Robert Kennedy and one each in five other victims.

Jimmy Breslin—claimed only 8 shots were fired despite the physical evidence of at least 9, four in Robert Kennedy and one each in five other victims.

Stanley Kawalac—claimed only 8 shots were fired despite the physical evidence of at least 9, four in Robert Kennedy and one each in five other victims.

Robert Ray Breshears—claimed only 8 shots were fired despite the physical evidence of at least 9, four in Robert Kennedy and one each in five other victims.

Thomas Perez—claimed only 8 shots were fired despite the physical evidence of at least 9, four in Robert Kennedy and one each in five other victims.

Marcus McBroom—indicated he saw a second gunman firing in the pantry. However, as the FBI files show, these statements have been misinterpreted, taken out of context or simply lack credibility due to inherent implausibility within them. Once more trotting out the angry lone-nut theory being completely supported by authorities. In 1986, nearly 20 years after the assassination, McBroom told a conspiracy writer that "…a man with a gun under his newspaper ran out in a very menacing way and me and a man by the name of Sam Strain and the man running the ABC camera we drew back instinctively when we saw the gun."

Evan Freed—indicated he saw a second gunman firing in the pantry. However, as the FBI files show these statements have been misinterpreted, taken out of context or simply lack credibility due to inherent implausibility within them. Once more trotting out the angry lone-nut theory being completely supported by authorities. Furthermore, his 1992 comments about a 'second man' are entirely consistent with the preponderance of evidence presented above, suggesting that Freed's 'second man' was actually Michael Wayne, a Sirhan look-alike.

Don Schulman—indicated he saw a second gunman firing in the pantry. However, as the FBI files show these statements have been misinterpreted, taken out of context or simply lack credibility due to inherent implausibility within them. Once more trotting out the angry lone-nut theory being completely supported by authorities. Immediately following the shooting Schulman was interviewed by Jeff Brent of Continental Broadcasting and said a security guard "had fired back." In 1971 Schulman said he did not see Sirhan shoot Kennedy, but he insisted that he saw the 'security guard' fire his gun. He also said he saw wounds erupting on Kennedy's body but refused to make any connection to the two events.

Booker Griffin—indicated he saw a second gunman firing in the pantry. However, as the FBI files show these statements have been misinterpreted, taken out of context or simply lack credibility due to inherent implausibility within them. Once more trotting out the angry lone-nut theory being completely supported by authorities.

Patricia Nelson—indicated she saw a second gunman firing in the pantry. However, as the FBI files show these statements have been misinterpreted, taken out of context or simply lack credibility due to inherent implausibility within them. Once more trotting out the angry lone-nut theory being completely supported by authorities.

Dennis Weaver—indicated he saw a second gunman firing in the pantry. However, as the FBI files show these statements have been misinterpreted, taken out of context or simply lack credibility due to inherent implausibility within them. Once more trotting out the angry lone-nut theory being completely supported by authorities.

Sam Strain—with Marcus Broom, who said, in 1986, nearly 20 years after the assassination, Marcus McBroom told a conspiracy writer that "...a man with a gun under his newspaper ran out in a very menacing way and me and a man by the name of Sam Strain and the man running the ABC camera we drew back instinctively when we saw the gun."

Joseph Klein—Dr. Fred S. Parrott told FBI agents that while he was standing outside the door to the Embassy Room, a man came by carrying a rolled-up newspaper under his arm followed by men shouting "Stop that man! Stop that man!" He described the man with the newspaper as a white male, dark complexion, dark hair, 25 to 27 years old, 5'7" tall, medium build. This description fits that of Michael Wayne who, at the time of the assassination, was a 21-year-old clerk at the Pickwick Bookstore in Hollywood and an avid collector of political memorabilia. After the shooting Wayne ran out of the pantry area and because someone shouted "Get him, he's getting away" security guard

Agustus Mallard grabbed him then put him in handcuffs. Wayne told police he was only running for a telephone to tell friends to turn on their television sets. He was interviewed by the LAPD but was never considered a suspect.

Other witness testimony has been used to support the presence of a second gunman in the pantry. However, it is clear from the FBI files that the person who these witnesses believed had carried a gun that night was actually Michael Wayne. Patricia Nelson and Dennis Weaver told FBI agents they believed they saw a man with a rolled-up newspaper or poster and that the wooden stock of a rifle had been protruding from it. However, they later stated they were likely mistaken and then identified the man as Michael Wayne. Nelson later identified Wayne from film footage of the hotel. "That's him. That's the same sweater, the same hair, the same sideburns", she told agents. She also identified the package as the one she saw. Weaver agreed with Nelson. Joseph Klein, who was with them at the time said, "That's him right there, I'm positive."

Michael Wayne had been photographed earlier in the evening by Bill Eppridge. Eppridge's photo shows RFK autographing Wayne's poster as the Senator walked to the Embassy Room to give his speech. Similar to John Lennon twelve years later, RFK was being more than kind to his possible eventual assassin.

For fifty-five years the government has used human error to build their case for a single shooter. Numerous researchers and others believe Thane Cesar murdered RFK. Why? Simply because Cesar was standing behind RFK at the time of the shooting, pulled his gun after RFK fell to the floor, was the only other person in the room known to have a gun and since has been identified as a CIA operative/asset. Don Schulman saw Cesar pull his gun and believes Cesar fired it. Sandra Serrano thought she heard a girl in a polka dot dress shout "We shot Kennedy." Some witnesses believed people running away from the scene of the crime were co-conspirators, but the police investigation proved that many of them were simply running to a telephone, seeking medical assistance, or evading gunfire. Some witnesses believed the girl in the polka dot dress and her companions were in the pantry during the shooting and were the only ones to flee the scene of the crime, thus rendering their actions suspicious. However, it has been proven that numerous others fled the pantry at the same time. The actions of Thane Eugene Cesar and Michael Wayne are very suspicious and should be investigated further by federal authorities. Robert Kennedy Jr., tried to interview Thane Eugene Cesar in the Philippines. At the last moment, Cesar demanded $25,000 in cash for the interview and would not admit any guilt regardless of the questioning. In September 2019 Thane Eugene Cesar died in the Philippines.

Although 77 people were supposedly in the pantry at the time of the assassination, this list includes others who may have been either in the pantry/kitchen or employees of the hotel who may have been in other areas adjacent to the pantry/kitchen. (f) The security of Robert Kennedy wasn't professional, and many people had access to the pantry/kitchen. It is unknown who was responsible for the security of the pantry. All indications lead to FBI agent William Barry. Whomever was responsible for security at The Ambassador Hotel that evening drastically failed.

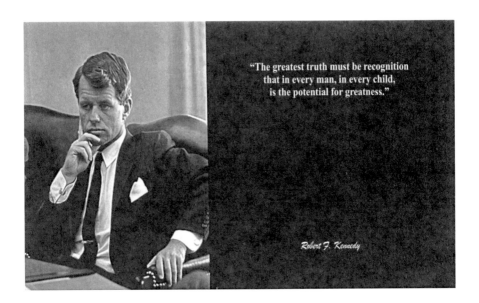

"The greatest truth must be recognition that in every man, in every child, is the potential for greatness."

Robert F. Kennedy

Ten

<u>Medical Reports on Robert F. Kennedy</u>

Unlike his brother, John, Robert Francis Kennedy had what is considered, 'the perfect autopsy.' This is no consolation to his family or friends, but unlike President Kennedy, RFK's autopsy proved irrefutable proof of a conspiracy. President Kennedy's mismanaged, contrived and shameful autopsy was intentionally fabricated and reported upon by similar forces (FBI, CIA, DPD) that chose to ignore the findings of intelligent, open-minded professionals who answered to no one, whose findings in RFK's autopsy were nonetheless blatantly ignored.

RFK's autopsy team was:

Dr. Thomas T. Noguchi, Chief Medical Examiner—Coroner
Dr. John E. Holloway, Deputy Medical Examiner
Dr. Abraham T. Lu, Deputy Medical Examiner

With Sirhan's defense team putting up no resistance, investigating nothing, failing to challenge any compelling evidence and interested in nothing other than to keep their client from going to the electric chair, the evidence in RFK's autopsy report would have, at a minimum, cleared Sirhan from being found guilty of murder. The most he could have been charged with, based on overwhelming evidence was conspiracy to commit murder since there was obviously at least one other gunman. It was blazingly apparent that Sirhan had no chance to reload his 8 shot revolver and also blatantly evident that somewhere between 10 and 14 shots were fired. Absolute proof of conspiracy. With the Three Stooges as his defense team, Sirhan was thrown to the wolves. The medical report that follows may be difficult to interpret, but three things are abundantly clear and were completely ignored by every individual and organization who should have exhausted any opportunity to discover the truth and chose by design not to. These truths are infallible. One, Sirhan approached RFK from the front, never getting close than 4 feet. Two, RFK was fatally wounded by a contact wound to the head, behind his right ear. Three, Sirhan Sirhan did NOT kill RFK. So, let us suggest something that should be abhorrent to anyone who ever held any modicum of trust in the U.S. Government: Anyone and everyone who investigated RFK's assassination and came to the conclusion that Sirhan Sirhan killed RFK:

      a.) lied their asses off!
      b.) were involved in the killing and subsequent cover-up!
      c.) were more than likely involved in JFK's assassination as well.

2nd rough draft,
edited 6/21/68 - JEH

"Dr. Holloway with dictation on the first composite gross protocol
for case 68-5731."

                 re-edited 7/18/68 by TTN and JEH.
                 re-edited 9/20/68 by JEH.

ANATOMICAL SUMMARY

GUNSHOT WOUND NO. 1 (FATAL GUNSHOT WOUND)

    ENTRY: Right mastoid region.

    COURSE: Skin of right mastoid region, right mastoid, petrous
              portion of right temporal bone, right temporal lobe,
              right cerebellum, and brain stem.

    EXIT: None.

    DIRECTION: Right to left, slightly back to front upward.

    BULLET RECOVERY: Fragments (see text).

GUNSHOT WOUND NO. 2, THROUGH-AND-THROUGH.

    ENTRY: Right axillary region.

    COURSE: Soft tissue of right axilla and right infraclavicular
             region.

    EXIT: Right infraclavicular region.

    DIRECTION: Right to left, back to front upward.

    BULLET RECOVERY: None.

GUNSHOT WOUND NO. 3.

    ENTRY: Right axillary region (just below Gunshot Wound No. 2
            entry).

    COURSE: Soft tissue of right axilla, soft tissue of right
            upper back to the level of the 6th cervical vertebra
            just beneath the skin.

    EXIT: None.

Autopsy Page 1.

DIRECTION: Right to left, back to front, upward.

BULLET RECOVERY: .22 caliber bullet from the soft tissue
                   of paracervical region at level of 6th
                   cervical vertebra at 8:40 A.M. June 6,
                   1968.

GUNSHOT WOUND NO. 1:

The wound of entry, as designated by Maxwell M. Andler, Jr, M.D.,
Neurosurgeon attending the autopsy, and more or less evident by
inspection of the apposed craniotomy incision, is centered 5
inches (12.7 cm) from the vertex, about 3/4 inch (1.9 cm) posterior
to the center of the right external auditory meatus, about 3/4 inch
(1.9 cm) superior to the Reid line, and 2-1/2 inches (6.4 cm)
anterior to a coronal plane passing through the occipital protuberance
at its scalp-covered aspect. The defect appears to have been about
3/16 inch (0.5 cm) in diameter at the skin surface. The surgical
incision passing through the area of the wound of entry has been
fashioned in a semilunar configuration with the concavity directed
inferiorly and posteriorly. The incision has been intactly sutured
by metallic and other material. The arc length is about 4 inches
(10 cm).

Further detailed description of the area is given in the Neuropathology portion of this report.

Varyingly moderate degrees of very recent hemorrhage are noted
in the soft tissue inferior to the right mastoid region, extending
medially, as well. There is no hematoma in the soft tissue.

In conjunction with the wound of entry, the right external ear
shows, on the posterior aspect of the helix, an irregularly
fusiform zone of dark red and gray stippling about one inch
(2.5 cm) in greatest dimension, along the posterior cartilaginous
border and over a maximum width of about 1/4 inch (0.6 cm) at
the midportion of the stippled zone. This widest zone of
stippling is approximately along a radius originating from the
wound of entry in the right mastoid region. Moderate edema
and variable ecchymosis is present in the associated portions
of right external ear as well.

GUNSHOT WOUND NO. 2:

This is a through-and-through wound of the right axillary, medial
shoulder, and anterior superior chest areas, excluding the thorax
proper. The wound of entry is centered 12-1/2 inches (13.6 cm)
from the vertex, 9 inches (22.9 cm) to the right of midline, and

Autopsy Page 2

212

3-3/4 inches (8.3 cm) from the back (anterior to a coronal plane passing through the surface of the skin at the scapula region). There is a regularly elliptical defect 3/16 x 1/8 inch over-all (about 0.5 x 0.3 cm) with thin rim of abrasion. There is no apparent charring or powder residue in the adjacent and subjacent tissue. The subcutaneous fatty tissue is hemorrhagic.

The wound path is through soft tissue, medially to the left, superiorly and somewhat anteriorly. Bony structures, major blood vessels and the brachial plexus have been spared.

The exit wound is centered 9-3/4 inches (about 24.5 cm) from the vertex and about 5 inches (about 12.5 cm) to the right of midline anteriorly in the infraclavicular region. There is a nearly circular defet slightly less than 1/4 inch x 3/16 inch overall (0.6 x 0.5 cm).

Orientation of the wounds of entry and exit is such that their major axes at the skin surfaces coincide with the central axis of a probe passed along the entirety of the wound path. No evidence of deflection of trajectory is found.

GUNSHOT WOUND NO. 3:

The wound of entry is centered 14 inches (35.6 cm) from the vertex and 8-1/2 inches (21.6 cm) to the right of midline, 2 inches (5 cm) from the back anterior to a plane passing through the skin surface overlying the scapula, and 1/2 inch (1.2 cm) posterior to the mid-axillary line. There is a nearly circular defect 3/16 inch by slightly more than 1/8 inch overall (0.5 x 0.4 cm). There is a thin marginal abrasion rim without evidence of charring or apparent residue in the adjacent skin or subjacent soft tissue. The subcutaneous fatty tissue is hemorrhagic.

The wound path is directed medially to the left, superiorly and posteriorly through soft tissue of the medial portion of the axilla and soft tissue of the upper back, terminating at a point at the level of the 6th thoracic vertebra as close as about 1/2 inch (1.2 cm) to the right of midline.

Bullet Recovery: A bullet of .22 caliber with lubaloy covering is recovered at the terminus of the wound path just described, at 8:40 A.M. June 6, 1968. There is a unilateral, transverse deformation, the contour of which is indicated on an accompanying diagram. The initials, TN, and the numbers 31 are placed on the base of the bullet for future identification. The usual Evidence envaolpe is prepared. The bullet, so marked and so enclosed as evidence, is given to Sergeant W. Jordan, No. 7167, Rampart Detectives, Los Angeles Police Department, at 8:49 A.M. this date for further studies.

Autopsy Page 3

ROUGH DRAFT   4   #68-573:
                               SENATOR ROBERT F. KENNEDY
                               JUNE 6, 1968

An irregularly bordered and somewhat elliptical zone of variably mottled recent ecchymosis is present in the superior-medial axillary skin on the right, in the zones of wounds of entry No. 2 and No. 3, especially the former. The ecchymosis measures 3-1/2 x 1-1/2 inches (9 x 3.8 cm) overall with the right upper extremity extended completely upward(longitudinally).

EXAMINATION OF CLOTHING AT TIME OF AUTOPSY:

1) There is a dark blue, fine worsted-type suit coat bearing the label "Georgetown University Shop - Georgetown, D.C". The coat has been cut and/or torn at the left yoke and left sleeve area. The right sleeve is intact. There is variable blood staining over the right shoulder region and on the right lapel. Two apparent bullet holes are identified in the right axillary region, slightly over 1 inch (2.5 cm) and slightly over 1-1/4 inch (3.2 cm) from the underseam area, respectively, and corresponding with wounds described on the body elsewhere in this report. Also noted at the top of the right shoulder region, centered about 1-1/4 inches from the shoulder seam and about 5/8 inch (1.6 cm) posterior to the yoke seam superiorly is an irregular rent of the fabric, somewhat less than 1/4 inch (3.2 cm) in diameter and definitely everting superficially and upward. The 3 front buttons of the garment are intact.

Subsequent examination of the coat showed the presence of a superficial through-and-through bullet path through the upper right shoulder area, passing through the suit fabric proper, but not the lining.

2) There is a pair of trousers of matching material with a very dark brown leather belt with rectangular metal buckle and showing the gold-stamped label "Custom Leather, Reversible, 32". The zipper is intact. Thre is a minimal amount of apparent blood staining over the anterior portions of the trouser legs.

3) There is a white cotton shirt with the label "K WRAGGE, 48 West 46th Street, New York". The laundry mark initials "RFK" are present on the neck band. The left portion of the shirt has been disrupted in approximately the same manner as the suit coat and is similarly absent. The right cuff is intact and is of semi-French design. A chain-connected yellow metal cufflink with plain oval design is in place. A corresponding left cufflink is not among the items submitted. Apparent bullet holes are identified as corresponding to those in the previously described area of suit coat.

4) There is a tie of apparent silk rep, navy blue with an approximately 3/16 inch (0.5 cm) grey diagonal stripe. The label is "Chase and Collier, McLean, Virginia". The maker is RIVETZ.

Autopsy Page 4

5)   There is a pair of navy blue, nearly calf length socks of
mixed cashmere and apparently nylon fiber, the fiber content
stencil labeling still being nearly discernible on the foot
portions.

6)   There is a pair of white broadcloth boxer type shorts with
two labels: "Sunsheen Broadcloth V'Cloth - 34; and "Custom
fashioned for Lewis and Thos. Saltz, Washington". There is a
small amount of blood stain at the anterior crotch, along with
pale straw colored discoloration to the left of the fly. A few
patches of dry blood are present on the back as well.

7)   There is a trapezoidally folded cotton handkerchief showing,
on what appears to be the presenting (anterior) surface, several
scattered dark red and somewhat brown spots ranging from a fraction
of a millimeter to about 4 mm (less than 3/16 inch) in greatest
dimension.

8)   No shoes are submitted for examination.

The above listed items are saved for further and more detailed
study by others.

GENERAL EXTERNAL EXAMINATION:

The non-embalmed body, measuring 70-1/2 inches (179 cm) in length
and weighing about 165 pounds (74.5 kg), is that of a well-developed,
well-nourished and muscular Caucasian male appearing about the
recorded age of 42 years. The extremities are generally symmetrical
bilaterally, showing no obvious structural abnormality.

The head shows extensive bandaging, somewhat blood-stained in the
posterior aspect. Dressings are also present in the right clavicular
region, the right axilla, and the right ankle regions. Also present
over the right inguino-femoral region are apparently elastoplast
dressings. A recent tracheostomy has been performed at a comparatively low level. A clear plastic tracheostomy tube fitted with
an inflatable cuff is in place. The area also shows a gauze
dressing.

Lividity is well developed in the posterior aspect of the body,
mainly at the upper shoulder and midback regions with approximately
equal distribution bilaterally. The lividity blanches definitely
on finger pressure.

Rigor mortis is not detected in the extremities or in the neck.

Rigor was noted to be developing in the arms and legs by the
time of conclusion of the autopsy.

Autopsy Page 5

A complete examination of the external surfaces of the body is udnertaken following removal of all dressings.

The head contour is generally symmetrical, due allowance being made for the soft-tissue edema and hemorrhage in the right post-auricular region in general. The hair is graying light brown and of male distribution. Calvity lines are well delineated on the scalp. Portions of the right half of the scalp have clipped and/or shaved. Hair in the inguinal and femoral regions has also been shaved in part. Hair texture is medium.

There is an irregularly bordered area of comparatively recent yet pale ecchymosis centered about one inch (2.5 cm) above the midportion of the right eyebrow. Marked ecchymosis with moderate edema is present in the right periorbital region but mainly of the upper eyelid. No abnormality is noted in the left periorbital tissue externally. No hemorrhage or generalized congestion is seen in the conjunctival or scleral membranes. The nose is symmetrical, showing no evidence of fracture or hemorrhage. The glabella shows no evidence of trauma.

Eye color is hazel. Pupillary diameters are equal at about 5 mm (3/16 in).

The buccal mucosa and the tongue show no lesion.

Chest diameters are within normal limits and there is bilateral symmetry. The breasts are those of a normal adult male. The abdomen is scaphoid. No abdominal scar is identified. There is an old low medial inguinal scar on the right.

Texture and configuration of the nails are within normal limits, and no focal lesions are noted. There is no peripheral edema.

The skin in general shows a smooth texture and no additional significant focal lesion. There is abundant sun tan, especially at the neck region where its contrast with the areas shaved for surgical preparation on the right can be noted. No evidence of powder burn, tattoo, or stippling is found in the area surrounding the wound of entry of Gunshot Wound No. 1, in an arbitrary circular zone to include the above-described stippling on the right ear, or beyond.

No structural abnormality is noted on the back.

There is a diagonally disposed recent surgical incision about 3 inches (7.5 cm) in length in the right anterolateral femoral region. This incision has been intactly sutured. There is an associated plastic tubing of small diameter, centered about 1/2 inch (12 mm) from the infero-medial margin of the incision.

Autopsy Page 6

ROUGH DRAFT   7   #68-5731
                              SENATOR ROBERT F. KENNEDY
                              JUNE 6, 1968

Also noted in a comparable location on the left are several
hypodermic puncture marks. These just-mentioned areas show
the presence of red-orange dye.

There are recent cutdowns at the right ankle and the lateral
right knee with thin polyethylene tubes in place. No extrava-
sation is noted.

The external genitalia are those of a normal circumcised adult
male.

CAVITIES:

Primary incision is first made as far as the two upper incisions,
allowing upward reflection of skin and soft tissue to afford
access for carotid angiography before the head is opened.
Following completion of these roentgenographic studies, the
traditional Y incision is continued. The peritoneal surfaces
are smooth and glistening. No free fluid is found in the
abdominal cavity. There are no adhesions. Abdominal organs
are in their usual relative positions.

The pleural surfaces are smooth. There is no pleural effusion.

The pericardium is intact and encloses a small amount of trans-
parent straw-colored liquid.

CARDIOVASCULAR SYSTEM:

The heart weighs 360 gm and presents smooth epicardial surfaces.
There is moderate right atrial dilatation. The contour otherwise is within normal limits. Cut surfaces of myocardium show
a uniform gray-red muscle fiber texture with no focal lesion.
The endocardial surfaces are smooth. About 50 ml of dark red
postmortem clot is present in the chambers collectively. No
cardiac anomaly is demonstrated. The thickness of the left
ventricular wall is up to 1.3 cm, and that of the right 0.3 cm.
Valve circumferences are: Tricuspid - 13, pulmonic - 8.5,
mitral - 10.5, and aortic - 7 cm. There are no focal lesions.
The coronary arterial tree arises in the usual sites and distri-
butes normally. The coronary arteries are thin-walled and pliable,
showing widely patent lumina. The aorta has a normal configuration
and varies from 3.3 to 5.2 cm in circumference. The intimal surface
of the aorta shows small and comparatively pale yellow atheromatous
areas totaling no more than 10% of the area studied.

The lining of the inferior vena cava is smooth throughout. The
distal end of the intravenous polyethylene catheter is noted at
the level of the 2nd lumbar vertebra and shows no evidence of
thrombosis at the tip. Free flow is also demonstrated.

Autopsy Page 7

Other vessels studied are not remarkable, save where special
descriptions are given elsewhere in this report.

RESPIRATORY SYSTEM:

The right lung weighs 490 gm; the left, 330 gm. There is
a moderate amount of wrinkling of the external surfaces,
suggestive of atelectasis. Dusky discoloration is noted
in the hypostatic portions bilaterally. The outer surfaces
of the lungs are intrinsically smooth. Cut surfaces of the
lungs disclose a few scattered areas of atelectasis, especially
in the left lower lobe. There is mild edema throughout. Hypostatic congestion is noted in an estimated 30% of the total
lung volume, approximately equally distributed bilaterally.
In these hypostatic areas there is probably patchy hemorrhage
of the matrix as well. No areas of consolidation are identified. Non-congested portions of the lungs are comparatively
pale tan in color. Anthracotic pigmentation is not excessive
for the age of the subject.

A small amount of slightly pink frothy mucoid material is
present in the bronchial tree, but no exudate. There is no
evidence of aspiration of gastric content.

The hilar lymph nodes show no abnormality.

NECK ORGANS:

The pharyngeal and laryngeal mucosa shows no focal lesion.
There are a few petechial hemorrhages of the epiglottis.
Intrinsic musculature and soft tissue of the larynx shows no
hemorrhage or other evidence of trauma. The vocal cords do
not appear edematous, nor is there evidence of generalized
submucosal edema. The hyoid bone is intact.

The trachea is in midline. The plastic tracheostomy tube
previously mentioned shows no obstruction of its airway and
no exudates or hemorrhagic material. The mucosa lining the
trachea is moderately injected at the general level of the
tracheostomy, again with no obvious exudate.

The thymus shows the usual atrophy and is comparatively fatty
but not otherwise remarkable.

HEPATOBILIARY SYSTEM:

The liver weighs 1810 gm and has a smooth intact capsule. The
edges are sharp. Cut surfaces of the liver show no focal lesion

Autopsy Page 8

in the comparatively dark brown matrix. Little blood wells
up from freshly cut surfaces. A number of normal sized portal
veins present themselves. There is no evidence of fibrosis.
No fatty sheen is seen on the cut surfaces.

The gallbladder has a wall of average thickness and a smooth
serosal surface. The organ is distended by the presence of
more than 25 ml of green-black bile of intermediate viscosity.
There are no calculi. The extrahepatic biliary system is patent.

HEMIC AND LYMPHATIC SYSTEM:

The 150 gm spleen is moderately firm and has a smooth intact
capsule. Multiple cut surfaces of the spleen show no focal
lesion in the dark gray-red matrix. The capsule shows no areas
of thickening. The malpighian bodies are distinct. No accessory
spleen is identified.

There is no evidence of marked departure from normal blood
volume. In areas where postmortem clot is found, this is of
uniformly normal degree and texture. No evidence of any
hemorrhagic diathesis is noted.

The abdominal lymph nodes, mainly the para-aortic, show moderate
enlargement (up to three times the normal size) but no induration
or focal change. Other lymph nodes studied are not remarkable.

PANCREAS:

Configuration and size are within normal limits. Multiple cut
surfaces show no evidence of an acute inflammatory change,
fatty necrosis, scarring, or hemorrhage.

UROGENITAL SYSTEM:

The right kidney weighs 180 gm and has a smooth capsule which
strips readily. Cut surfaces disclose normal corticomedullary
ratios, with an average cortical thickness of about 6 mm,
compared with 1.0 cm of the medulla. There are no focal lesions.
A moderate amount of engorgement is noted.

The left kidney weighs 175 gm and has a generally smooth capsule
which can be stripped readily. Also present, however, is a
retention cyst about 2.5 cm in greatest dimension but showing,
on subsequent study, a principal volume delineated by a space
2.0 x 1.8 x 1.5 cm. Thin watery liquid is enclosed. About
3.0 cm from one pole of the left kidney and 2.0 cm from the pelvis,

Autopsy Page 9

is a well-circumscribed and slightly raised subcapsular nodule
having a uniform yellow matrix and measuring 1.0 x 0.9 x 0.9 cm
overall. The cut surface of this yellow nodule protrudes slightly.
The lesion is about 6.0 cm from the just-described retention cyst.
Intervening matrix of the left kidney shows no focal change. The
renal pelves of both kidneys and both ureters show no induration,
dilatation, or exudates. Ureteral implantation is noted to be
normal in the urinary bladder. About 8 ml of faintly amber-pink
cloudy urine is contained. There is no focal lesion of the
urothelial lining. There are no urinary calculi.

The prostate is symmetrical with a transverse diameter of 3.5 cm.
Cut surfaces show no distinct nodular areas and no focal lesion.
there are scattered areas of vascular engorgement near the origin
of the prostatic urethra. A slightly gritty texture is found
on the cut surfaces of the prostate. Scattered discrete calculi
up to 2 mm in diameter are found.

The seminal vesicles are of normal configuration and contain a
small amount of green-gray mucoid material.

Both testes are present in the scrotal sac and are of normal
size and consistence. Tubular stringing is readily accomplished.
No evidence of hydrocele is present.

DIGESTIVE SYSTEM:

The esophagus is lined by smooth pale-gray epithelium following
the usual longitudinal folds. No focal lesion is found. The
stomach has a wall of average thickness and a smooth serosal
surface. There is mild gaseous dilatation. No evidence of
hemorrhage or ulceration is found in the gastric mucosa. Within
the lumen is about 500 ml of cloudy gray watery mucoid material
in which no discrete food fragments are found. A small amount
of hemorrhagic material is inadvertently admitted into the gastric
content as the latter is secured for possible toxicological
studies. The duodenum, small intestine, and colon show no gross
abnormalities of mucosal or serosal elements. The mesenteric
lymph nodes are not remarkable.

ENDOCRINE ORGANS:

The pituitary is intrinsically symmetrical and within the normal
limits of size, as is the sella turcica.

The thyroid is symmetrical and not enlarged; cut surfaces of
the brown-red colloid matrix shows no focal change.

Autopsy Page 10

The adrenals total 13.5 gm and are of normal configuration.
Multiple cut surfaces show no focal lesion. The thickness of
the cortex is little more than one millimeter. The medullary
tissue is not remarkable.

MUSCULOSKELETAL SYSTEM:

The bony framework is well developed and well retained. No
evidence of a diffuse osseous lesion is found. The fracture
of the right orbital plate and of other components of the base
of the skull are described in detail elsewhere in this report,
mainly the Neuropathology section. No additional evidence of
recent fracture or other focal trauma is demonstrated in the
skeleton.

The clinically described and radiologically documented old
fractures are not dissected.

The vertebral marrow is a uniform brown-red, showing no focal
change.

Cut surfaces of muscles studied, in areas apart from the trauma,
show no abnormality.

HEAD AND NERVOUS SYSTEM:

Additional features revealed by reflection of the scalp include
a fairly well demarcated area of non-recent hemorrhagic discoloration, about 1.5 cm in greatest dimension, in the left
parietal-occipital region. No associated galeal hemorrhage is
demonstrated.

A complete description of the brain in situ and following removal,
before and after fixation, will be found elsewhere in this report.

The cerebrospinal fluid is blood tinged.

Abundant and freshly clotted but drying blood is found at the
right external auditory canal, extending outward to the lateral
interstices of the external ear. No evidence of hemorrhage is
found at the left ear.

The spinal cord is taken for further evaluation by the Neuro-
pathologist. At time of removal of the cord, a small amount of
cervical epidural hemorrhage is noted. There is no evidence, on
preliminary inspection, of avulsion of roots leading to the right
brachial plexus.

Autopsy Page 11

ROUGH DRAFT   12   #68-5731
                             SENATOR ROBERT F. KENNEDY
                             JUNE 6, 1968

Those portions of peripheral nervous system exposed by the extent
of dissection indicated above in general show no abnormality.

SPECIMENS SUBMITTED:

Organs and body fluids enumerated elsewhere in this report, for
the purpose of toxicological examinations.

Tissue sections for microscopic examination as denoted in other
portions of this report.

Other specimens for special studies as described in accompanying
reports.

COMPLETION OF AUTOPSY:

The above-described dissections, postmortem radiographic studies,
the autopsy photographs, and the placing of retained specimens in
suitably labeled containers, were all completed by 9:15 A.M., this
date. The body was then released to the embalmers who had arrived
to perform their functions.

THOMAS T. NOGUCHI, M.D.
CHIEF MEDICAL EXAMINER-CORONER

JOHN E. HOLLOWAY, M.D.
DEPUTY MEDICAL EXAMINER

ABRAHAM T. LU, M.D.
DEPUTY MEDICAL EXAMINER

JEH::AMJ::C
9/25/68

Autopsy Page 12

CERTIFICATE OF DEATH
STATE OF CALIFORNIA—DEPARTMENT OF PUBLIC HEALTH

7097-021970

1A. NAME OF DECEASED—FIRST NAME: Robert	1B. MIDDLE NAME: Francis	1C. LAST NAME: Kennedy	DATE OF DEATH—MONTH, DAY, YEAR: June 6, 1968	2A. HOUR: 1:44 AM

3. SEX: M	4. COLOR OR RACE: White	5. BIRTHPLACE: Brookline, Mass.	6. DATE OF BIRTH: 11/20/25	7. AGE: 42 YEARS

8. NAME AND BIRTHPLACE OF FATHER: Joseph P. Kennedy   Boston, Mass.
9. MAIDEN NAME AND BIRTHPLACE OF MOTHER: Rose Fitzgerald   Boston, Mass.

10. CITIZEN OF WHAT COUNTRY: U.S.A.
11. SOCIAL SECURITY NUMBER: 026-24-0879
12. MARRIED, NEVER MARRIED, WIDOWED, DIVORCED: married
13. NAME OF SURVIVING SPOUSE: Ethel Skakel

14. LAST OCCUPATION: U.S. Senator
15. NUMBER OF YEARS: 4 years
16. NAME OF LAST EMPLOYING COMPANY OR FIRM: United States Government
17. KIND OF INDUSTRY OR BUSINESS: Government

PLACE OF DEATH

18A. PLACE OF DEATH—NAME OF HOSPITAL OR OTHER IN PATIENT FACILITY: Good Samaritan Medical Center
18B. STREET ADDRESS: 1212 Shatto Street
18C. INSIDE CITY CORPORATE LIMITS: yes

18D. CITY OR TOWN: Los Angeles
18E. COUNTY: Los Angeles
18F. LENGTH OF STAY: 10 days / 10 days

USUAL RESIDENCE

19A. USUAL RESIDENCE—STREET ADDRESS: 870 United Nations Plaza
19B. INSIDE CITY CORPORATE LIMITS: yes
20. NAME AND MAILING ADDRESS OF INFORMANT: Ethel S. Kennedy

19C. CITY OR TOWN: New York
19D. COUNTY: New York
19E. STATE: New York
Same as 19A

PHYSICIAN'S CORONER'S CERTIFICATION

21A. CORONER: INVESTIGATION—
Thomas Noguchi M.D. June 6, 1968
CORONER—LOS ANGELES COUNTY
ADDRESS: THOMAS T. NOGUCHI, M.D.
LOS ANGELES, CALIFORNIA

FUNERAL DIRECTOR AND LOCAL REGISTRAR

22A. BURIAL: Burial
22B. DATE: 6-8-68
23. NAME OF CEMETERY OR CREMATORY: Arlington Nat. Cem.
25. NAME OF FUNERAL DIRECTOR: Columbia Family
27. LOCAL REGISTRAR SIGNATURE
JUN 8 1968

CAUSE OF DEATH

29. PART I. DEATH WAS CAUSED BY:
(A) GUNSHOT WOUND OF RIGHT MASTOID PENETRATING BRAIN
(B)
(C)

30. PART II. OTHER SIGNIFICANT CONDITIONS:
OPERATION: YES

INJURY INFORMATION

33. SPECIFY ACCIDENT, SUICIDE OR HOMICIDE: HOMICIDE
34. PLACE OF INJURY: HOTEL
35. INJURY AT WORK: NO
36A. DATE OF INJURY: JUNE 5, 1968
36B. HOUR: 12:15 AM

37A. PLACE OF INJURY: 3400 WILSHIRE BLVD., LOS ANGELES
37B: 3000
38: NO

40. DESCRIBE HOW INJURY OCCURRED: SHOT BY KNOWN PERSON

STATE REGISTRAR
A. B. C. D. E. F. X

THIS IS A TRUE CERTIFIED COPY OF THE RECORD FILED IN THE LOS ANGELES COUNTY HEALTH DEPARTMENT IF IT BEARS THE SEAL IMPRINTED IN PURPLE INK.

JUN 6 1968

JUNE 1968
LOS ANGELES

56-156-261

original in IA

RFK Death Certificate.

223

No matter what Sirhan's involvement in RFK's assassination was, it is acknowledged by anyone with some semblance of intelligence who has looked even with mild interest at the evidence that Sirhan fired at RFK but did not kill him. Dr. Noguchi, an avowed expert in such matters concluded that RFK was killed by a single fatal shot—a contact wound fired up close, behind his right ear. In the military, and in the parlance of any professional assassin, a "double tap" is the preferred method of execution. Sirhan was never behind RFK, which means someone else—the true assassin—was. The forces who claimed to investigate RFK's murder marched forward with one goal, to vilify and crucify Sirhan Sirhan as the lone assassin. Shame on the American public for letting them perpetuate this preposterous falsehood and not demand accountability for those responsible.

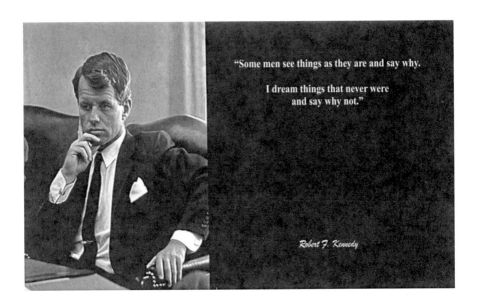

"Some men see things as they are and say why.

I dream things that never were
and say why not."

Robert F. Kennedy

Eleven

RFK's Eulogy by Edward Kennedy

On June 8, 1968, at 10:00 a.m., Edward Moore Kennedy delivered the following eulogy for his third fallen brother, Robert Francis Kennedy at St. Patrick's Cathedral in New York City.

"Your Eminences, Your Excellencies, Mr. President:

On behalf of Mrs. Kennedy, her children, the parents, and sisters of Robert Kennedy, I want to express what we feel to those who mourn with us today in this Cathedral and around the world.

We loved him as a brother, and as a father, and as a son. From his parents, and from his older brothers and sisters—Joe and Kathleen and Jack—he received an inspiration which he passed on to all of us. He gave us strength in time of trouble, wisdom in time of uncertainty, and sharing in time of happiness. He will always be by our side.

Love is not an easy feeling to put into words. Nor is loyalty, or trust, or joy. But he was all of these. He loved life completely and he lived it intensely.

A few years back, Robert Kennedy wrote some words about his own father which expresses the way we in his family felt about him. He said of what his father meant to him, and I quote:

What it really all adds up to is love—not love as it is described with such facility in popular magazines, but the kind of love that is affection and respect, order and encouragement, and support. Our awareness of this was an incalculable source of strength, and because real love is something unselfish and involves sacrifice and giving, we could not help but profit from it.

Beneath it all, he has tried to engender a social conscience. There were wrongs which needed attention. There were people who were poor and needed help. And we have a responsibility to them and to this country. Through no virtues and accomplishments of our own, we have been fortunate enough to be born in the United States under the most comfortable conditions. We, therefore, have a responsibility to others who are less well off.

That is what Robert Kennedy was given. What he leaves to us is what he said, what he did, and what he stood for. A speech he made to the young people of South Africa on their Day of Affirmation in 1966 sums it up the best, and I would like to read it now:

There is discrimination in this world and slavery and slaughter and starvation. Governments repress their people; millions are trapped in poverty while the nation grows rich, and wealth is lavished on armaments everywhere. These are differing evils, but they are the common works of man. They reflect the imperfection of human justice, the inadequacy of human compassion, our lack of sensibility towards the suffering of our fellows. But we can perhaps remember—even if only for a time—that those who live with us are our brothers; that they share with us the same short moment of life; that they seek—as we do—nothing but the chance to live out their lives in purpose and happiness, winning what satisfaction and fulfillment they can.

Surely, this bond of common faith, this bond of common goal, can begin to teach us something. Surely, we can learn, at least, to look at those around us as fellow men. And surely, we can begin to work a little harder to bind up the wounds among us and to become in our own heart's brothers and countrymen once again. The answer is to rely on youth—not a time of life but a state of mind, a temper of the will, a quality of imagination, a predominance of courage over timidity, of the appetite for adventure over the love of ease. The cruelties and obstacles of this swiftly changing planet will not yield to the obsolete dogmas and outworn slogans. They cannot be moved by those who cling to a present that is already dying, who prefer the illusion of security to the excitement and danger that come with even the most peaceful progress.

It is a revolutionary world we live in, and this generation at home and around the world has had thrust upon it a greater burden of responsibility than any generation that has ever lived. Some believe there is nothing one man or one woman can do against the enormous array of the world's ills. Yet many of the world's great movements, of thought and action, have flowed from the work of a single man. A young monk began the Protestant reformation; a young general extended an empire from Macedonia to the borders of the earth; a young woman reclaimed the territory of France; and it was a young Italian explorer who discovered the New World, and the 32-year-old Thomas Jefferson who claimed that all men are created equal.

These men moved the world, and so can we all. Few will have the greatness to bend history itself, but each of us can work to change a small portion of events, and in the total of all those acts will be written the history of this generation. Each time a man stands up for an ideal, or acts to improve the lot of others, or strikes out against injustice, he sends forth a tiny ripple of hope, and crossing each other from a million different centers of *energy and daring, those ripples build a current that can sweep down the mightiest walls of oppression and resistance.*

Few are willing to brave the disapproval of their fellows, the censure of their colleagues, the wrath of their society. Moral courage is a rarer commodity than bravery in battle or great intelligence. Yet it is the one essential, vital quality for those who seek to change a world that yields most painfully to change. And I believe that in this generation those with the courage to enter the moral conflict will find themselves with companions in every corner of the globe.

For the fortunate among us, there is the temptation to follow the easy and familiar paths of personal ambition and financial success so grandly spread before those who enjoy the privilege of education. But that is not the road history has marked out for us. Like it or not, we live in times of danger and uncertainty. But they are also more open to the creative energy of men than any other time in history. All of us will ultimately be judged, and as the years pass, we will surely judge ourselves on the effort we have contributed to building a new world society and the extent to which our ideals and goals have shaped that event.

Our future may lie beyond our vision, but it is not completely beyond our control. It is the shaping impulse of America that neither fate nor nature nor the irresistible tides of history, but the work of our own hands, matched to reason and principle, that will determine our destiny. There is pride in that, even arrogance, but there is also experience and truth. In any event, it is the only way we can live.

That is the way he lived. That is what he leaves us.

My brother need not be idealized, or enlarged in death beyond what he was in life; to be remembered simply as a good and decent man, who saw wrong and tried to right it, saw suffering and tried to heal it, saw war, and tried to stop it.

Those of us who loved him and who take him to his rest today, pray that what he was to us and what he wished for others will someday come to pass for all the world.

As he said many times, in many parts of this nation, to those he touched and who sought to touch him:

Some men see things as they are and say why. I dream things that never were and say why not."

Senator Ted Kennedy gives his brother's eulogy, St. Patrick's Cathedral.

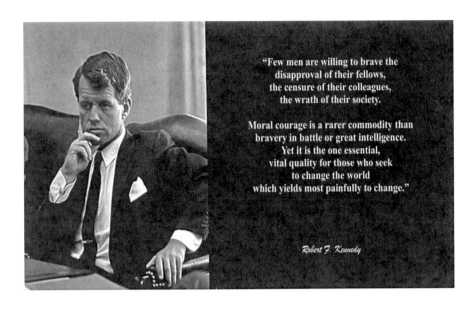

"Few men are willing to brave the
disapproval of their fellows,
the censure of their colleagues,
the wrath of their society.

Moral courage is a rarer commodity than
bravery in battle or great intelligence.
Yet it is the one essential,
vital quality for those who seek
to change the world
which yields most painfully to change."

Robert F. Kennedy

Twelve

<u>Funeral Train</u>

On June 8, 1968, a 21-car train carrying the body of slain New York Senator and Presidential candidate Robert F. Kennedy left from New York's Penn Station headed to Washington D.C.'s Union Station. Over a century earlier, a similar train transported the body of President Lincoln from Washington D.C. to his Springfield, Illinois home. Presidents Grant, Garfield, McKinley, Franklin D. Roosevelt and Eisenhower took similar trips.

During his brief 82-day campaign for the Democratic nomination, Robert F. Kennedy traveled to some of the poorest regions of the United States supporting striking farm workers, the poor, the disenfranchised and spoke in support of the anti-Vietnam war movement. RFK was the only white politician in America who could walk through the streets of both white and black working-class neighborhoods and be embraced by both. His sincerity was readily apparent.

With Dr. King viciously silenced, Kennedy became the voice of poor people—black and white—the only national leader who commanded respect and enthusiasm. Kennedy believed that convincing poor people of all colors to pursue their shared class interests offered the only solution to the deep racial hostility currently tearing the nation apart. "We have to convince the Negroes and poor whites that they have common interests," he told journalist Jack Newfield. He continued, "If we can reconcile those two hostile groups, and then add the kids, you can really turn this country around." Like his brother before him, he had the ideas, the vision and the resolve to change the United States—just not the time and Government support to implement these ideas.

"I think I cried all the way from L.A. to Atlanta, I kept saying to myself, what is happening in America? To lose Martin Luther King and to lose Robert Kennedy two months later...it was too much."

John Lewis, former U.S. Representative from Georgia and long-time civil-rights leader who was a Kennedy adviser and was with RFK the night he was shot.

"I had a rosary in my shirt pocket,
and I took it out thinking that he would
need it a lot more than me.

I wrapped it around his right hand
and then they wheeled him away."

Juan Romero
Busboy who was shaking hands
with Robert Kennedy when he was shot.

"No one came after him who could speak simultaneously
for the unemployed black teenager and the white worker
trapped in a dead-end job and feeling misunderstood."

Jack Newfield, journalist

"Inside the train, you couldn't hear anything.
But on the platform,
you could hear the cheers, and people crying."

Art Buchwald

"We were well-represented on the outside of the train.
That's where all my people were."

Millie Williams, RFK staffer
with Coretta Scott King, two of only
five African Americans on the train.

*"I wish this thing could go through every state,
Just keep going...I didn't want it to end."*

Dave Powers
Special Assistant to JFK.

"He was our last hope.
He was the one to carry the torch.
After losing Medgar, JFK, Malcolm, Dr. King
and now Bobby.

I think as a country, we all died
a little on June 6."

Hosea Williams
Remarks on hearing Robert Kennedy's death.

*"What kind of a President would he have made?
I think very likely a greater one than JFK.
He was more radical than JFK,
he understood better the problems of the excluded groups,
and he would have been coming along
in a time more propitious for radical action."*

Arthur Schlessinger
Special Assistant to JFK.

"I for one find it unacceptable and worse than no answer
at all to be told that all of us collectively are to blame
and that ours is a sick society.
Perhaps we are sick, but not in the way they mean it.
We are sick with grief, sick with anger and
sick of what's been allowed to go on
in this nation for a long time."

Ronald Reagan, Governor of California in 1968
and 40th President of the United States.

"The death of Robert Kennedy was a terrible blow
to the people of this Nation and the World.
As a champion of the poor,
of the victims of injustice,
and of reconciliation and peace,
he was an apostle and a symbol of hope.

He felt deeply and aroused deep feelings.
He is still mourned, and he is remembered as he was.
Passionate, moral, committed, spontaneous, joyful."

Jimmy Carter
39th President of the United States.

"He embodied the whole message
of the faith of his father and mother.

Before His Holiness Pope Francis
called us to engage in a culture of encounter,
he visually, instinctively lived the life of encounter.
The life of the outstretched hand,
not the clenched fist."

Bill Clinton
42nd President of the United States.

"His interest in minorities' causes may have helped or harmed his campaign, but it was one of the principals he stood for. No other white person could have made the remarks in Indianapolis after Dr. King's assassination than Bobby. His willingness to be challenged on his actions and beliefs. His pursuit of politics out of a sense of obligation, rather than out of a 'lust' for power."

Johnny Carson
Host of The Tonight Show
June 7, 1968.

*"Standing on the back of a flatbed truck at 17th & Broadway,
he (RFK) spoke for seven minutes.
As moving as his speech that night in
cold and drizzly Indianapolis had been,
it elicited little commentary afterward.
Like Dr. King's equally memorable remarks the
night before—his last speech,
the one about having been to the mountaintop—it
was lost in the enormity of the assassination.
But in Room 306 of the Lorraine Motel,
Kennedy's words were duly noted."*

Ralph David Abernathy
On RFK comments after MLK assassination
April 4, 1968.

"Kennedy could never replace King.
But to his (MLK) disciples back at the Lorraine Motel that night,
and throughout the black community,
he (RFK) had picked up the torch.

There was but one question about that torch.
How long Bobby Kennedy would get to hold it.
I don't know, I almost feel like somebody said.

He's probably going to be next.
I can't remember that but that was
the feeling that many of us had."

Andrew Young
Politician, close friend to Martin Luther King.

*"I don't weep often, but today,
I wept for my country."*

Reverend Billy Graham

"You know, I have almost never been
able to cry about Martin
because I couldn't permit myself to...but now,
I don't have to restrain myself,
and I can't control my feelings."

Coretta Scott King
regarding Robert Kennedy's death.

*"The Church is a marvelous thing at a time like this.
It's really at its best only at the time of death.
The rest of the time it's often rather silly—little men
running around in their black suits.
But the Catholic Church understands death."*

Jacqueline Kennedy Onassis
remarks to Frank Mankiewicz after
he announced Robert Kennedy's death.

"The body left here today with a planeload
of family, friends, staff, including
Mrs. John Kennedy and Mrs. Martin Luther King.

So, in one airplane,
three widows of three American public
figures murdered by assassins."

David Brinkley
The Huntley-Brinkley Report

"There was grief...I remember looking
back down the aisle just after the plane
had left the Los Angeles airport.
One of the Kennedy aides in back of us was crying."

George Plimpton
June 6, 1968

"He's mad at what happens in this country.
He does not know whether this is the act of a
single person or if this is the act of a conspiracy.
But from him, one got the impression—it's
no more than that—there's kind of a pattern.
Faceless men—that's the phrase I heard."

Sander Vanocur, NBC News
on flight back with Robert Kennedy's body
discussing the actions of Edward Kennedy who
remained constantly beside his slain brother the entire flight,
just like Jackie with JFK from Dallas.

"My brother need not be idealized,
or enlarged in death beyond what he was in life;
to be remembered simply as a good and decent man,
who saw wrong and tried to right it,
saw suffering and tried to heal it, saw war, and tried to stop it.

Those of us who loved him and who take him to his rest today,
pray that what he was to us and what he wished for others
will someday come to pass for all the world.
As he said many times, in many parts of this nation,
to those he touched and who sought to touch him:

Some men see things as they are and say why.
I dream things that never were and say why not."

Ted Kennedy
Eulogy for Bobby earlier in the day

One can't help but wonder if there are enough tears in the world to wash away the sins of mankind. Our greatest liability as a people is our ability to use our intelligence against each other. There is an inexplicable, innate evil hidden deep within our human frailty that most of us – without knowledge or intent – manage to keep dormant. But there are also those among us who seem to thrive by bringing it to the surface, by nurturing it and using it to exact and inflict pain and suffering, all intended to promote their own evil agendas. These are the people who will perpetually wage war against martyrs like RFK, JFK, MLK and others.

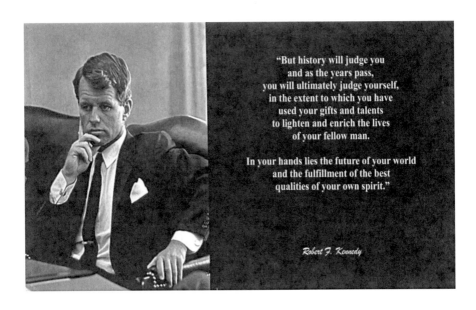

"But history will judge you
and as the years pass,
you will ultimately judge yourself,
in the extent to which you have
used your gifts and talents
to lighten and enrich the lives
of your fellow man.

In your hands lies the future of your world
and the fulfillment of the best
qualities of your own spirit."

Robert F. Kennedy

Thirteen

<u>What May Have Been</u>

This Chapter is a discussion by the authors. Our thoughts pursuant to the impact of the deaths of visionaries including JFK, RFK, MLK and others, and what the world – and the United States – may have looked like had they all remained alive to realize their dreams.

The United States and the world changed for the worsening with JFK's assassination on November 22, 1963. As a country, we lost not only our innocence, but also our faith in government institutions. Unfortunately, the forces, individuals and agencies that were responsible for JFK's death were just taking batting practice in the planning stages for the atrocities that would follow. Five months prior to his death, on the very night JFK gave his groundbreaking Civil Rights speech, Medgar Evers was killed in his driveway shortly after midnight on June 12, 1963 in front of his entire family. The person who was charged with Evers murder was Byron De La Beckwith.

After watching Kennedy's Civil Rights speech that evening, Beckwith, an avowed white supremacist, calmly loaded his rifle and went to the neighborhood where Medgar Evers lived. Evers was the embodiment of everything that was wrong in Beckwith's twisted mind. Evers worked as the field secretary for the NAACP and was also a spokesman for the Civil Rights Movement and its peaceful quest for racial equality. Beckwith's case went to trial in 1964 but the jury was deadlocked. A second trial later that year resulted in another deadlocked jury. Both juries were made up entirely of white males.

When a 1989 newspaper investigation revealed evidence that a Mississippi state agency had committed jury tampering in 1964, Myrlie Evers pushed for a new trial for Beckwith. His friends called Beckwith 'DeLay' and he certainly lived up to his nickname when he was arrested again in 1990. Since he had previously experienced mistrials, not an acquittal, he could not be saved by double jeopardy.

His trial began in January 1994 and although in public Beckwith had consistently denied shooting Evers, privately he bragged about killing 'that nigger.' On February 5, 1994,

'DeLay' Beckwith proudly displaying his white supremacist views.

Beckwith was convicted of Evers' murder. He received a life sentence. His lawyers argued for an appeal based upon him being denied the right to a speedy trial. They were unsuccessful. On January 21, 2001, De La Beckwith died after he was transferred from prison to the University of Mississippi Medical Center in Jackson, Mississippi. He was 80 years old. He had suffered from heart disease, high blood pressure, and other ailments for some time. More details on Jowers will be discussed in the Epilogue chapter.

The Evers family waited 30 years for justice. Thirty years of freedom that Beckwith enjoyed with his family that Medgar Evers never had the opportunity to enjoy. Medgar was only 37 years old when he was brutally murdered in his driveway. Had Medgar lived, he would have been able to retire at sixty-five and possibly enjoy grandchildren. As author Brennan's Father was often prone to say (we hope in jest!), "Life is mean, cruel and indifferent!"

It has been fifty-five years since Robert Kennedy was assassinated in Los Angeles. In 2023, he would have been 98 years old. His mother, Rose, lived until 104 so it is possible RFK could still be alive, enjoying his eleven children and numerous grandchildren. Like his Brother before him, the forces, people, and agencies were stepping back into the batter's box for round five. Gone already were Medgar Evers, JFK, Malcolm X, and Dr. Martin Luther King, Jr.

In baseball, it's three strikes and you're out. In life, all it takes is one strategic bullet and carefully deigned plans to hide the truth. The planners of all of these murders are smug, self-satisfied and smiling that they all pulled off their unthinkable executions and skated away. All a person has to do is look at the

LBJ being sworn in as President by Judge Sarah Hughes (polka dot dress!)

The infamous 'Wink and a Smile' photo suppressed by the FBI until 1999.

image taken fifteen seconds after LBJ was sworn in as President aboard Air Force One to see the smiles, winks, and enjoyment on the faces of the winning team. The photo taken after LBJ's swearing in ceremony was hidden from the American public until 1999, after both Jackie Kennedy and John Jr. were both dead. This chapter endeavors to imagine what the United States, as well as the world, may have been had the forces of darkness not taken control over our country's hierarchy, control and power they still wield today.

Most researchers and historians believe that Robert Kennedy would have won the 1968 Presidential election. It is hard to state with certainty everything that may have changed in the United States and the world in the past 55 years but there is no doubt that had JFK lived to serve two terms and Bobby two more terms afterwards many historical events probably would not have occurred. The Vietnam war would have ended in 1964, saving tens of thousands of American lives. LBJ would have gone to prison and died in disgrace. The CIA would have been dismantled or had their power severely curtailed. Hoover would have been forced to retire when he turned 70. The civil unrest and riots of 1968 may never have happened. More than likely there would have been no anti-war riots in Chicago at the Democratic National Convention. No Kent State killings in 1970. No Watergate tapes and for that matter, no Richard Nixon as President. Had Bobby lived, it's even possible that Teddy Kennedy may not have suffered his own personal and political nightmare at Chappaquiddick. If Teddy didn't have the death of Mary Jo Kopechne as a noose around his neck, who is to say that after Robert served two terms as President, that Teddy wouldn't have been elected in 1976 and served two terms? Had those scenarios played out, not only would we not have Nixon as President but more than likely you could rule out the Presidencies of Ford, Carter, and Reagan. It's within the realm of possibility to imagine that there would have been no pardon of Richard Nixon, no un-elected VP or President Ford, nor Jimmy Carter's disastrous four years in office. If we eliminate Ronald Reagan, there would be no Iran-Contra and all the drug wars which occurred while Reagan was in office. Under the Reagan/Bush administration we were basically supplying the Contras with weapons in exchange for their drugs to introduce crack cocaine and help finance Afghanistan in its struggle against the Soviet Union. If there was no Reagan Presidency, it is unlikely that George H.W. Bush would have ever become President. In this scenario, we wouldn't have experienced the Reagan assassination attempt or had a former CIA Director as President. There would have been no Gulf War. Without 'Poppa Bush' there would be no 'Dubya.' Without George Walker Bush there is no 9/11, and no wars with Iraq, Iran, or Afghanistan all undertaken so 'Dubya' could control his oil interests in the Gulf of Emirates. The enormity and impact of this scenario on The United States and in fact the entire world is nothing short of stunning.

We are not suggesting that a 19-year run of Kennedy leadership would have been perfect, but it is safe to say that RFK was well on his way to becoming President before the same vicious cabal that cut his Brother down eliminated RFK as well, for many of the same reasons but ultimately to perpetuate their greedy, power-grabbing intentions. Who knows how the United States and the world could have changed? JFK's vision of peace on earth, goodwill towards men could have become a reality. One common thread that was instilled in the Kennedy brothers from a very young age by their father was service to this country. Not just military service, but political office as well. All of the Kennedy children had trust funds that made Joe and Rose's children millionaires on their 18th birthday. There was no reason for them to serve in politics to distort the system and become rich, they were already rich. As JFK said in his inaugural address, "If a free society cannot help the many who are poor, it cannot save the few who are rich."

As Edward said in his eulogy of Bobby, "My brother need not be idealized, or enlarged in death beyond what he was in life; to be remembered simply as a good and decent man, who saw wrong and tried to right it, saw suffering and tried to heal it, saw war, and tried to stop it." Teddy would continue, "Some men see things as they are and say why. I dream things that never were and say why not." The very foundation that the Kennedy brothers stood on was a platform of helping those who were not as fortunate as them, not just here in the United States but around the world. They had to know their father, Joseph P. Kennedy, had made the majority of his money during prohibition, but they were not raised to be elitists. They were raised to serve and be compassionate to others.

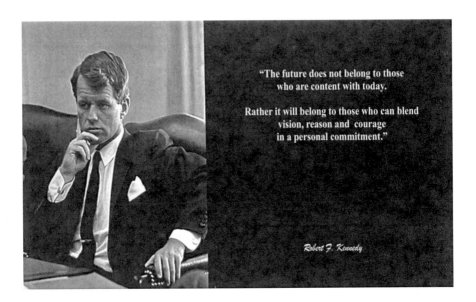

"The future does not belong to those
who are content with today.

Rather it will belong to those who can blend
vision, reason and courage
in a personal commitment."

Robert F. Kennedy

Fourteen

<u>Afterword</u>

In the first of our series, 'JFK—Marked For Death,' we examined individuals and agencies who had the means, motive, and opportunity to kill JFK. More importantly, we also discussed what they had to lose had JFK been elected to a second term.

With Robert Kennedy, we chose to detail his run for the Presidency, his assassination, and the charade of an investigation which followed. There was no true investigation, only deception and hearsay, all intended for the result they wished for: Sirhan Sirhan singled out as the lone assassination. The same cabal that eliminated JFK also removed RFK. Hence our subtitle, "Another Son Sacrificed." Although we don't discuss each person or agency by chapter, RFK had many of the same enemies who conspired to assassinate JFK. Bobby satirically called himself 'Senator Ruthless.'

Had RFK won the Presidency in 1968 and continued with his brother's agendas, there would be people and agencies who would have wanted him dead. Certainly, the Mafia since he had prosecuted more Mafia leaders as Attorney General than anyone before him. It is certain that RFK would appoint an Attorney General to carry on that initiative. Since ending the Vietnam war was crucial to Bobby's campaign platform, the American Military Industrial Complex would have had their own reasons for wanting RFK out of the way. They wanted the war in Vietnam and knew LBJ would follow their orders. Although based on real events, Oliver Stone's 1991 movie, 'JFK,' has LBJ signing NSAM 273 (to increase U.S. military presence in Vietnam) as he says, "Just get me elected...I'll give you your damn war." Texas Big Oil was concerned if RFK became President he would have either repealed or severely cut the Oil Depletion Allowance Tax, costing them millions of dollars. But who else might have wanted Bobby dead?

The answer is crystal clear: the same individuals and organization that made certain that JFK would never live to serve another term. RFK had every intention of scheduling a true investigation into his brother's death. RFK Jr. recently announced that his father felt that the Warren Commission report was a "shoddy piece of craftmanship." He continued, "He publicly supported the Warren Commission Report but privately he was dismissive of it." Bobby didn't believe in the Warren Report and as President could have 'hand-picked' his own panel to investigate. This would have given him the power to subpoena all the original members for their testimony. We already know that Richard Russell, John Sherman Cooper, and Hale Boggs publicly criticized the original report. One can only imagine what they may have disclosed before Allen Dulles and Gerald Ford had been questioned. The United States would have seen an uprising against the Government that we hadn't seen since the Civil War, and rightfully vindicated at the same time.

All of the same people and agencies that wanted JFK dead would also want Bobby out of the way. The FBI, the CIA, the American Military Industrial Complex and the U.S. Media. The Secret Service were not responsible for Presidential candidates (until Bobby's death), so they had no involvement like they did in Dallas. Like the Dallas Police, the LAPD had to have key figures involved from the beginning. The standard operating procedure was the same. Deny, deny, deny, lie, lie, lie and then cover-up any mistakes that may have been made. Which leaves us with only two other people that we discussed in our previous book "JFK—Marked For Death." Lee Oswald and Lyndon Baines Johnson. Obviously, Oswald was dead, but he didn't kill JFK, nor did Sirhan kill RFK, he wasn't the killer of a Kennedy. Which leaves us with LBJ.

Could the man leaving office affect the person coming into office? Unequivocally, yes. LBJ was happy when Robert Kennedy left the justice department to run for the Senate seat in New York. He even helped him with his campaign. Not out of friendship, out of politics. LBJ knew he would pick up another Senate vote (although RFK did vote against LBJ on occasions and despite that privately the two men despised each other). Once LBJ decided not to run again in 1968, he immediately started supporting his Vice President, Hubert Humphrey, much like Humphrey had curried favor with LBJ in 1964.

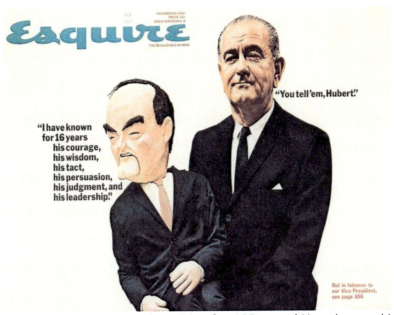

Esquire Magazine, November 1964 after LBJ named Humphrey as his VP.

Lyin' Lyndon did not want RFK to be President...for a myriad of reasons. As President RFK would still be in position to have LBJ sent to prison for extortion and bribery due to his illegal activities with Bobby Baker and Billie Sol Estes. He didn't want his administration examined, nor his Warren Commission members subpoenaed. He didn't want the Vietnam War to end since he was benefitting financially the longer the war waged on. LBJ was still highly motivated financially for war. Irrefutably involved in JFK's assassination could LBJ have been involved with Bobby's murder? He still had the motive, means, and opportunity. LBJ despised RFK, and the feeling was mutual. Despite failing health, LBJ did not want to spend the rest of his life in prison, and in our opinion, this was his biggest motivation for helping to eliminate Bobby. Revenge is a dish that is best served cold, just like Lyndon's heart. In 1968, he still had deep connections with the same evil cabal who assassinated his Brother.

We, as authors, plan to do a series of 'Marked For Death' books because we know the U.S. Government has been lying to us for decades. In future books we hope to cover topics such as:

Malcolm X
Dr. Martin Luther King Jr.
Iran Contra/Barry Seal
The Atlanta Child Murders
Ronald Reagan's assassination attempt
Princess Diana &
John F. Kennedy Jr.

The most controversial of these topics would be John F. Kennedy Jr. Everything we've been told regarding his murder, not a plane crash. Author Gary Fannin knew one of JFK Jr.'s best friends, Joe Perry Barlow. During their discussion he disclosed JFK, Jr's political intentions, including a run for the Senate seat in New York in 2000. If that had been successful, he would have run for the Presidency in 2004. Of course, we know who won those elections. They would not allow someone as vibrant, intelligent, good-looking and carrying the Kennedy name to stop their agendas, political or otherwise.

So much of the John F. Kennedy Jr. plane crash is a blatant lie told by the U.S. Government and so easily proven. They claimed he was an inexperienced pilot who didn't have flight instrument rating for flying at night. Wrong! He had nearly 2,500 hours of experience, he just hadn't taken the test. They claimed he flew over the dark Atlantic. Wrong! He followed the coastline all the way until he was forced over the Atlantic for the last twenty minutes of the flight. They claimed the weather was horrible, poor conditions, low visibility. Wrong! Anyone can simply go to the NOAA website and see the weather was perfect. They claimed his plane spiraled out of control and he became disoriented. Wrong! He called into the tower at Martha's Vineyard airport six minutes before his plane's tail exploded, then he lost control of the aircraft. LIES, LIES, and even more LIES.

Today, government lies are pervasive, and the American media their obsequious puppets. We intend to disclose the most egregious of their lies. We will be publishing a series of 'Marked For Death' books because we know the U.S. Government has been lying to us for decades. We hope you will support our lifelong cause.

Gary Fannin   Tim Brennan
June 2023   June 2023

Epilogue

Absolute Power Corrupting Absolutely; Government, Media and Big Pharma

In addition to the assassinations of RFK, JFK, MLK and others the following is a list of political assassinations that were orchestrated and approved at the highest levels of the United States government since 1957. Who makes these types of decisions, what gives them the right to conduct these activities on foreign soil with apparent impunity, why doesn't the rest of the civilizied world howl in protest and what did the United States (and the world) gain?

Carlos Castillo Armas—July 26, 1957, Guatemala
Patrice Lumumba—January 17, 1961, Republic of the Congo
Ngo Dinh Diem—November 2, 1963, South Vietnam
Ngo Dinh Nhu—November 2, 1963, South Vietnam
Hasan Ali Mansur—January 26, 1965, Iran
Salvador Allende—September 11, 1973, Chile

These men paid the highest price with their lives. But the CIA and the American Military Industrial Complex are not content with murder, they want complete control of other countries. Below is a list of coup d' etats cleverly orchestrated by Allen Dulles and the CIA.

Mohammad Mosaddegh—August 19, 1953, Iran
Jacobo Arbenz—June 27, 1954, Guatemala

In addition to those two coup d'états, the United States was heavily opposed to Salvador Allende becoming President of Chile. Declassified documents show that from 1962-1964, the CIA spent

$3 million on anti-Allende propaganda and an additional $2.6 million to finance the campaign of his rival, Eduardo Frei.

In September 1970, President Nixon informed the CIA that an Allende government was unacceptable and authorized an additional $10 million to stop him from coming to power or to unseat him. A recently released CIA document declared, "It is firm and continuing policy that Allende be overthrown by a coup."

On November 5, 1970, Secretary of State Henry Kissinger wrote a memo to President Nixon to discuss the National Security Council's agenda with Salvador Allende. The subject line specifically addresses the November 6 meeting to 'consider the question of what strategy we should adopt to deal with an Allende Government in Chile.' Kissinger clearly states in the memo that, 'the consolidation of Allende in power in Chile, therefore, would pose some very serious threats to our interests (money) and position in the hemisphere, and would affect developments and our relations to them elsewhere in the world.' He continues, 'U.S. investments (totaling some one billion dollars) may be lost, at least in part; Chile may default on debts (about $1.5 billion) owed the U.S. Government and private banks. What were we really buying?" JFK once remarked, "The cost of freedom is always high—and Americans have always paid it." What is the cost of truth and why is it so difficult to admit to?

On August 26, 1998, Janet Reno, U.S. Attorney General directed the Civil Rights Division of the United States Department of Justice, assisted by the Criminal Division, to investigate two separate, recent allegations related to the April 4, 1968 assassination of Dr. Martin Luther King Jr. She assigned civil rights special counsel Barry Kowalski, who previously prosecuted the Los Angeles police officers in the Rodney King beating, to review the allegations. These allegations were brought forward by Loyd Jowers, a former Memphis tavern owner and white supremacist, and Donald Wilson, a former FBI agent.

MEMORANDUM

THE WHITE HOUSE
WASHINGTON

November 5, 1970

MEMORANDUM FOR THE PRESIDENT

FROM: Henry A. Kissinger

SUBJECT: NSC Meeting, November 6 -- Chile

This meeting will consider the question of what strategy we should adopt to
deal with an Allende Government in Chile.

A. DIMENSIONS OF THE PROBLEM

The election of Allende as President of Chile poses for us one of the most
serious challenges ever faced in this hemisphere. Your decision as to
what to do about it may be the most historic and difficult foreign affairs
decision you will have to make this year, for what happens in Chile over
the next six to twelve months will have ramifications that will go far beyond
just US-Chilean relations. They will have an effect on what happens in
the rest of Latin America and the developing world; on what our future
position will be in the hemisphere; and on the larger world picture, including our relations with the USSR. They will even affect our own con-
ception of what our role in the world is.

Allende is a tough, dedicated Marxist. He comes to power with a profound
anti-US bias. The Communist and Socialist parties form the core of the
political coalition that is his power base. Everyone agrees that Allende
will purposefully seek:

-- to establish a socialist, Marxist state in Chile;

-- to eliminate US influence from Chile and the hemisphere;

-- to establish close relations and linkages with the USSR, Cuba
and other Socialist countries.

The consolidation of Allende in power in Chile, therefore, would pose some
very serious threats to our interests and position in the hemisphere, and
would affect developments and our relations to them elsewhere in the world:

-- US investments (totaling some one billion dollars) may be lost, at least
in part; Chile may default on debts (about $1.5 billion) owed the US
Government and private US banks.

November 5, 1970 Kissinger document regarding Allende in Chile.

Most Americans are not aware that Martin Luther King's family
filed a civil suit in 1999 to force more information into the public eye,

and in response a Memphis jury ruled that the local, state, and federal governments were liable for King's death. After the verdict was read, Coretta Scott King said, "There is abundant evidence of a major, high-level conspiracy in the assassination of my husband." She continued, "The jury found the Mafia and various government agencies were deeply involved in the assassination. Mr. Ray was set up to take the blame."

Loyd Jowers in Civil Suit court.

In 1993, Jowers appeared on the ABC News program, 'Prime Time Live' and claimed to be part of a conspiracy to kill Dr. King involving the Mafia and the U.S. government. According to Jowers, the alleged assassin, James Earl Ray, was a scapegoat, and was not responsible for King's murder. Jowers said he was paid $100,000 to arrange the assassination by Mafioso Frank Liberto as a favor to a Mafia friend. He admitted there were numerous alleged assassins, including Raoul, named by James Earl Ray, as well as Memphis police Lt. Earl Clark, who Jowers said he hired to fire the fatal shot from behind his tavern, 'Jim's Grill,' on the brushy hillside below the Ray rooming house.

In 1998, Agent Wilson alleged that shortly after MLK's assassination he took a small envelope containing papers from the abandoned car of James Earl Ray in Atlanta and concealed them for 30 years. These papers allegedly contained references to Raoul and other figures associated with the assassination of President Kennedy. According to Wilson, someone who later worked in the Clinton White House subsequently stole the papers he took from Ray's car, including one with the telephone number of the Atlanta FBI office.

Wilson told his story to the District Attorney in Atlanta and stated that he would provide the documents to the Department of Justice for a full investigation. However, there were only two documents which remained from the stolen envelope. One of the documents was a portion of a torn page from a 1963 Dallas Texas telephone directory, including the telephone numbers of Jack Ruby and oil billionaire H.L. Hunt. The other document was a piece of paper with two handwritten columns, the first of words and the second of numbers. Both documents have handwritten entries with the name Raul (both spellings, Raoul).

The civil suit found Jowers, local, state, and federal governments liable for King's death and awarded the King family the $100 in damages they had sought, which they then donated to charity. "This was never about the money, it was a chance to rewrite history," said Dexter Scott King. He continued, "This is the period at the end of the sentence. So please, after today, we don't want questions like, 'Do you believe James Earl Ray killed your father?' No, I don't, and this is the end of it." Dexter wasn't the only person to believe there had been a conspiracy to kill his father, JFK, RFK and other political leaders in the 1960's.

"I think there was a major conspiracy to remove Dr. King from the American scene," said Rep. John Lewis (D-GA), a civil rights icon. "I don't know what happened, but the truth of what happened to Dr. King should be made available for history's sake." Andrew Young, former U.N. ambassador and Atlanta mayor who was at the Lorraine Motel with Dr. King when he was shot agreed. "I would not accept the fact that James Earl Ray pulled the trigger, and that's all that matters."

Of course, the U.S. government will always continue to deny the truth and their role in rewriting history. After the trial, the U.S. government's favorite mouthpiece against history, Gerald Posner was interviewed. Posner had just published, 'Killing the Dream: James Earl Ray and the Assassination of Martin Luther King, Jr.,' which was intentionally published on the anniversary of Dr. King's murder, April 4, 1999, merely seven months before the Jowers civil trial started. Posner stated after the trial, "The Memphis trial would be a footnote, at best, in the tangled history of the King case." Posner then told The New York Times, "It distresses me greatly that the legal system was used in such a callous and farcical manner in Memphis. If the King family wanted a rubber stamp of their own view of the facts, they got it."

In 2010, Posner was accused of multiple accounts of plagiarism while he was the chief investigative reporter at 'The Daily Beast.' Allegations of plagiarism also surfaced in his books, 'Miami Babylon, Secrets of the Kingdom and Why America Slept.' Posner hired attorney/author Mark Lane to represent him against the Miami New Times on grounds that its investigation and reporting of this case damaged Posner's business relationship with his publishers and caused him emotional distress. Of course, with Mark Lane representing him, he won. Afterwards in a press release, Posner stated, "Although I'm convinced Lee Harvey Oswald assassinated President Kennedy, I've always believed that had Mark Lane represented Oswald, he would have won an acquittal. That's why Mark Lane was the obvious choice as my own attorney." This is the same Mark Lane that Marguerite Oswald hired in 1963 to represent her accused dead son, Lee Harvey Oswald, before the Warren Commission. Lane's representation was denied. The Warren Commission tried to twist Mark Lane's words and called him as a witness to the JFK assassination. He informed them he was not a witness but was simply representing Lee Harvey Oswald before the Commission. Again, his requests were denied, even though lawyers were allowed to represent dead Nazi soldiers during the Nuremberg trials.

Posner still wasn't in the clear. On May 3, 2013, he was named in a federal lawsuit brought by Harper Lee in New York City. Lee claimed her literary agent's son-in-law, Samuel Pinkus, tricked her into signing away her rights to 'To Kill a Mockingbird.' She claimed the royalties were to be paid into a corporation formed by Gerald Posner specifically for that purpose. This case never went to trial as Posner and another defendant settled with Lee out of court and were dismissed from the lawsuit. Yet, as of this writing in 2023, if the government wants to disprove any conspiracy theory, all they have to do is place a microphone in front of their paid CIA puppet, Gerald Posner.

We are not trying to throw Gerald Posner under the bus. His actions are thoroughly notated on his Wikipedia page with the excuses that he was the 'wrong person at the wrong time.' In fact, author Fannin has personally met Posner and he is a likable guy. He just always defends the U.S. Government regardless of the evidence proving otherwise. If we truly wanted to throw anyone under the bus it would be the U.S. government. Even on their webpage, www.justice.gov, they continue to slander everyone involved with the King v. Jowers trial. Although a Memphis jury ruled in favor of the King family, the website has these statements listed about the trial.

"*Based upon an assessment of Wilson's professed disdain for the FBI and his conduct, his inconsistent statements, and all other available facts, his claim that he discovered papers in Ray's car is not credible. Accordingly, we have concluded that the documents do not constitute legitimate evidence pertaining to the assassination.*"

The justice.gov website continues:

"Because the uncorroborated allegations regarding Raoul originated with James Earl Ray, we ultimately considered Ray's statements about him. Ray's accounts detailing his activities with Raoul related to the assassination are not only self-serving, but confused and contradictory, especially when compared to his accounts of activities unrelated to the assassination. Thus, Ray's statements suggest that Raoul is simply Ray's creation. For these reasons, we have concluded there is no reliable evidence that a Raoul participated in the assassination."

All good, except for the fact there is court testimony in the original James Earl Ray trial and the King v. Jowers trial in which the jury agreed to the testimony. Do we not have the right to be judged by a jury of our peers? If our peers (or members of the jury) disagree with the official government narrative, does this make them wrong? Yes, in the eyes of the U.S. government. As Hitler once said, "the bigger the lie, the more people will believe it."

"In sum, the evidence admitted in King v. Jowers to support the various conspiracy claims consisted of inaccurate and incomplete information or unsubstantiated conjecture, supplied most often by sources, many unnamed, who did not testify. Because of the absence of any reliable evidence to substantiate the trial's claims of a conspiracy to assassinate Dr. King involved the federal government, Dr. King's associates, Raoul, or anyone else, further investigation is not warranted."

The last line of the previous paragraph strikes a nerve already seriously frayed. 'Further investigation is not warranted.' This sounds eerily similar to the House Select Committee on Assassinations when they said there had been a conspiracy to assassinate President Kennedy and Dr. King and recommended the Justice Department investigate further in 1979. As of this writing, 44 years later, The Justice Department has chosen to do absolutely nothing.

The Hitler statement, "the bigger the lie, the more people will believe it," should be added to the Presidential oath of office. The oath is found in Article II of the Constitution. It contains 35 words and says:

"I (name) do solemnly swear (or affirm) that I
will faithfully execute the Office of
President of the United States,
and will to the best of my ability, preserve, protect
and defend the Constitution of the United States."

According to ABC News, George Washington reportedly added the words, "so help me God" to the oath, and it has been spoken by every President since then with the exception of Theodore Roosevelt.

These 35 words are so popular, they are mentioned in Disney's 'Hall of Presidents.' What we are suggesting (in jest, even though it seems so appropriate!) is to eliminate the "so help me God" tag line and replace it with an updated version of Hitler's line, "we will tell even bigger lies, and force the American public to believe it." This is obviously humor, but it has been enforced on us already.

During Ronald Reagan's Presidency, at his first cabinet meeting he asked all the department heads to state their agenda for the next four years. CIA Director William Casey said, "We'll know our disinformation program is complete, when everything the American public believes is false."

"We'll know our disinformation program is complete when everything the American public believes is false."

William Casey, former CIA Director
from a staff meeting in 1981

The Death of Free Media in America

As incredulous as this sounds, we, as a nation, believe very little of the national news that is presented to us on a daily basis. Sadly, this disinformation campaign goes all the way back to when the CIA was created in 1947. At that time, however, it was much easier for the American people to swallow the minnow compared to the whale we are asked to swallow now. In 1947, there were only three television networks, along with radio, national magazines and newspapers. Today there are hundreds of television networks, thousands of other media outlets and a plethora of social outlets via the Internet. Big changes to communication outlets were enacted in 1996.

The Communications Act of 1934 was the statutory framework for U.S. communications policy, covering telecommunications and broadcasting. This 1934 Act basically created the FCC, the agency formed to implement and administer the economic regulation of the interstate activities of the telephone monopolies and the licensing of spectrum used for broadcast and other purposes…whew! Basically, it allowed for any individual to own up to five media outlets, whether they were television stations, radio, or print.

On February 8, 1996, President Bill Clinton signed the Telecommunications Act of 1996, one of the worst decisions of his Presidency. This law represented a major change in American telecommunications because it was the first time that the internet was included in broadcasting. Not that regulating the internet is wrong, it's what the rest of the law allowed. This law allowed anyone to enter any communications business, to let any communications businesses compete in any market against any other. The legislation's primary goal was deregulation of the converging broadcasting and telecommunications markets. (Ask Ronald Reagan how the deregulation of air traffic controllers worked for his administration!) Essentially what this law created was fewer, but larger corporations to operate more media enterprises within a sector and to expand across media sectors, through cross-ownership rules, thus enabling massive and historic consolidation of media in the United States. In layman's terms, it allowed six corporations to influence all the media information we receive.

Study the charts on the following pages of the six LARGE corporations that own over 90% of the media and see if you can find a network, magazine, or newspaper that you watch or read that isn't influenced by these six corporations. Also, let's compare their salaries and revenues compared to others.

To completely put this into perspective, we have to look at the analytics prior to the Telecommunications Act of 1996.

In 1983, 90% of all media
was owned by 50 companies...today it is owned by six.

232 Media Executives control the
information of 277 million people.
Today, 1 Executive = 850,000 People.

Total revenue by the six corporations
$275,900,000,000
Or
$36,000,000,000 more than Finland's GDP!
Enough to buy EVERY NFL TEAM 12 TIMES!

5X the amount of the 2008 Government
Bailout of General Motors!

The Big Six control 70% of all cable on television
Nearly 17 hours a day and
Control 11 Major Markets across the U.S.!

178,000,000 users read Time Warner monthly!
More than double Digg, Reddit, & Tumbler combined!
Almost 3X as much as Google!

News Corp owns the top newspaper on 3 Continents.
The Wall Street Journal, The Sun, The Australian.

In 2010, they avoided paying $875,000,000 in U.S. taxes.
Or
Twice FEMA's annual budget.
Could fund NPR for 40 years.

In 1995, the FCC forbade companies to own
more than 40 radio stations.
Today, Clear Channel owns over 1200!
In fact, in Minot, ND, THEY OWN THEM ALL!

The Big Six's Box Office sales in 2010:
$7,000,000,000!
That's 2X the box office sales
of the next 140 studios combined.

AOL spent $124,000,000,000
to buy Time Warner in 2001.
That's 6X what Congress funded to rebuild Iraq.

Thanks to President Bill Clinton, the FCC deregulation and decades-long orgies of mergers and acquisitions, these six giant corporations will continue to control 90% of everything Americans see, hear, read, or consider important. Start thinking for yourself. The Dumbing Down of America is well underway, and the CIA is conducting the orchestra!

In addition to the political assassinations of the 1960's, there is probably no darker day in American history than September 11, 2001. Also, sadly, much of what Americans have been told regarding 9/11 is a media lie.

The 9/11 Commission was established by President George 'Dubya' Bush on November 27, 2002, 442 days after the attacks. Their conclusions were eventually published in The Final Report of the National Commission on Terrorist Attacks Upon the United States.

The Commission interviewed over 1,200 people, reviewed over 2,500,000 pages of documents, including classified national security documents. In addition to identifying intelligence failures that occurred before the attacks, the report provided evidence of the following:

- Airport security footage of the hijackers as they passed through airport security.

- Excerpts from the United Airlines Flight 93 cockpit voice recording, which recorded the sounds of the hijackers in the cockpit and the passengers' attempts to regain control.

- Eyewitness testimony of passengers as they described their own final moments to family members and authorities on satellite phones and cellphones from the cabins of the doomed airliners.

- Television/video of planes hitting the World Trade Center Buildings 1 & 2 and the Pentagon.

We will attempt to address some of the anomalies of the above four statements. We also want to emphasize we do not want to write about individual family members and what horrors the families of all the victims had to endure. In fact, co-author Tim Brennan worked with Todd Beamer's father. Todd was on Flight 93 and was famous for saying, "Let's Roll" in an attempt to overtake the plane from the hijackers.

Before we take a closer look at the four statements, let us not fail to mention that months before 9/11 an FBI field agent sent a letter to his Director expressing concern over the number of Arab Americans that were taking flying lessons. The letter was never acted upon.

The first statement: Airport security footage of the hijackers as they passed through security gates. Yes, there was footage of the hijackers going through security, but it's the documents these hijackers were carrying that were amazingly found intact at the crash sites that is nearly impossible to believe. We were told that four of the hijackers' passports survived in whole or in part after three of the four crashes. Two were recovered from the crash site of United Airlines Flight 93 in Pennsylvania. These belonged to Ziad Jarrah and Saeed al Ghamdi. One belonged to a hijacker on American Airlines Flight 11. This was the passport of Satam al Suqami. A passerby picked it up and gave it to a NYPD detective shortly before the World Trade Center towers collapsed. A fourth passport was recovered from luggage which did not make the connecting flight of American Airlines Flight 11. This passport belonged to Abdul Aziz al Omari. Of the four scenarios just presented, the last one is the only one in which there is a remote possibility of it actually occurring.

Statements two and three: The U.S. media wants us to believe there was a passport found at the crash site of United Airlines Flight 93 in Shanksville Pennsylvania. The following are images from the crash site.

Flight 93 crash site.

In the photo on the previous page, we cannot even determine if there is a plane involved in this crash photo. Even in the photo below, it is hard to see images of a plane, yet somehow two passports have survived the intensity of the fire and crash and were used to identify two of the hijackers.

Expanded view of Flight 93 crash site.

Aerial view of Flight 93 crash site.

In the second image on the previous page, we can clearly see the tail section of the aircraft. There are no other images that resemble any part of an airplane. The National Transportation Safety Board's flight path study of United Airlines Flight 93, dated February 19, 2002, provides further information. The following are the key details of the flight.

- United flight 93 departs Newark at 8:42 a.m. and reaches its cruising altitude of 35,000' at 9:02 a.m.

- at 9:28 a.m., the words, "get out of here" were recorded on the air traffic control radio at FAA's Cleveland facility.

- At 9:34 a.m., the plane climbs to 41,000.'

- At 9:39 a.m., the plane starts descending at 4,000' per minute.

- At 9:41 a.m., the radar stations stopped receiving transponder information.

- At 9:59 a.m., the airplane is at 5,000.'

- At 10:02 a.m., the airplane is at 10,000.'

- At 10:03:11 a.m., the airplane crashes at 563 mph in an inverted 40-degree angle.

At 9:41 a.m., the FAA stopped receiving transponder information from the plane. This could have been explained simply as the hijacker's turning this feature off so that they could not be seen on radar. However, the flight data recorders were recovered from the accident. They indicated that when Flight 93 crashed there was about

37,500 pounds of fuel remaining. The crash occurred at 10:03 a.m., yet the entire fire was extinguished in under three hours.

In 2023, on average, the maximum usable range of a cell tower was 25 miles. Typical coverage radius of a cell tower is 1-3 miles in dense urban environments and can be as little as one-quarter to a mile before handing off a user's connection to the next cell site. In rural Shanksville Pennsylvania, we could assume at best, but doubtful, there were cell towers every 25 miles in 2001. According to the 9/11 Commission Report, passengers were making phone calls to their families on satellite phones (carrier provided) and their cell phones.

The following diagram would show the distance of the cell phone towers in relation to an airplane flying above.

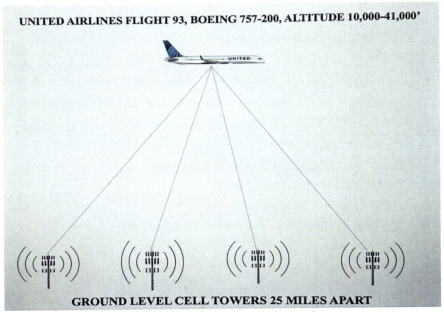

Graph showing UA Flight 93 and cell towers on ground.

Here comes the tricky part, mathematics. If an airplane is traveling 500 Miles Per Hour, it is traveling approximately 733 feet per second. With cell towers 25 miles apart, this would allow a maximum of three minutes before the signal would move to the next cell phone tower. Also, we must consider the altitude of the plane between 10,000 and 41,000 feet. These are the altitudes described on the FAA report. Using the same calculations, if the cell towers were five miles apart, there would only be 36 seconds between cell tower signals to an airliner possibly up to 41,000' above! If the cell towers were only one mile apart, there would only be seven seconds between cell tower signals. Even by 2023 standards, these scenarios are highly unlikely, thereby making those supposed numerous calls unlikely.

By the time Flight 93 had turned back toward Washington, D.C., we knew the country was under attack, and that Flight 93 was in the hands of hijackers. It's probable target was The White House. At some point, Vice President Dick Cheney, in the Presidential Emergency Operations Center deep under the White House, authorized Flight 93 to be shot down. Without authorization, two Air National Guard pilots, Lieutenant General Marc Sasseville and Heather Penney, scrambled into F-16's that were unarmed, prepared to take Flight 93 down by whatever means necessary, including using their own planes as weapons. Flight 93 went down in Shanksville before Sasseville and Penney could take it down themselves. There are still many who think Flight 93 was actually shot down by our own Government, and the fact that the debris field covered eight miles would support this theory. It's highly unlikely we'll ever know the true story.

Statement four: The television and video cameras of the World Trade Center and the Pentagon. We will start with the Pentagon crash. According to the 9/11 Commission Report, American Airlines Flight 77 left Dulles airport at 8:20 a.m. At 8:51 a.m., the attackers stormed the cockpit and forced the passengers and crew to the rear of the cabin. Two passengers discreetly made cell phone calls to family members on the ground. (see previous diagram). The plane crashed into the western side of the Pentagon at 9:37 a.m. According to the 9/11 Commission report, the plane suffered severe damage and caused a large fire that took several days to extinguish.

Amazingly, this fire took days to extinguish however the fire in Shanksville was extinguished within three hours. When the plane hit, a portion of the Pentagon it collapsed immediately, and five additional stories collapsed at 10:17 a.m. The following images are taken from an AP video on YouTube. The first image is four seconds into the film. The second image is also four seconds into the film, but a white oval is highlighted to show the green grass and blue sky. The next two images are from five seconds into the film.

View of Pentagon from AP video. Note time of four seconds bottom left.

View of Pentagon from AP video. Note time of five seconds bottom left.

White line now appears in image.

Now look at the highlighted images one second apart.

View of Pentagon from AP video. Note time of six seconds bottom left.

View of Pentagon from AP video. Note time of seven seconds bottom left.

Official FBI released photo immediately after the Pentagon attack. Where did the airplanes wings disappear to?

Where is the airplane?

Aerial view...note lack of airplane?

Close-up from ground...move it along, nothing (airplane) to see here.

Herve Villechaize, "Da Plane, Da Plane," where's the DAMN plane?

Overhead view of Pentagon collapse. Again, where are the airplane wings?

The day before the 9/11 attacks, Donald Rumsfeld, the Secretary of Defense gave a nationally televised speech from the Pentagon. He stated, "The topic today is an adversary that poses a threat, a serious threat, to the security of the United States of America." He continued, "Perhaps this adversary sounds like the former Soviet Union, but that enemy is gone. The adversary's closer to home. It's the Pentagon bureaucracy. Not the people, but the processes. Not the civilians, but the systems. Not the men and women in uniform, but the uniformity of thought and action that we too often impose on them. The technology revolution has transformed organizations across the

"The national security threat posed by military bureaucratic inefficiency and waste"

**Speech by
Donald Rumsfeld
10 September 2011**

private sector, but not ours, not fully, not yet. We are, as they say, tangled in our anchor chain. Our financial systems are decades old. According to some estimates, we cannot track $2.3 trillion in transactions. We cannot share information from floor to floor in this building because it's stored on dozens of technological systems that are inaccessible or incompatible."

Once the United States was attacked (by us!), the $2.3 trillion comment and story disappeared. Why? Because the records that Donald Rumsfeld talked about were stored in the exact area where the plane crashed into the Pentagon. The largest government building in the world and the terrorists were smart enough to know exactly where to crash their missile...er, airplane.

According to Architects & Engineers for 9/11 Truth, there are numerous discrepancies in the official 9/11 Commission Report. Experienced airline pilot, Daryl Hoover said, "Very experienced pilots all said that trying to fly a plane at 550 knots (633 MPH) at or very near sea level was exceeding the maximum stress level of the aircraft by 100+ knots (115 MPH). An inexperienced pilot who only flew and failed flying Cessnas would never be able to fly a 757 so close to the ground and that the turn he made to hit the Pentagon (550 knot descending turn) would stress the structure to the point of breaking up." He continued, "The engines and gear struts would have certainly been visible after the crash. Where are they in the photographs?"

The videos of the two planes striking the twin towers of the World Trade Center are incomprehensible to watch, knowing that so many people perished. However, YouTube video of World Trade Center building #7 again proves media complicity. Jane Standley of the BBC reported that World Trade Center building #7 had collapsed 20 minutes before it actually did! The following image is from the video with WTC #7 standing behind her. How did she know it was going to collapse? The National Institute of Standards and Technology claimed that embers ignited a fire which then caused the 47-story building to collapse on itself at 5:20 p.m., hours after the initial incident occurred that morning.

World Trade
Center Building #7

TERRORISM ATTACKS IN US

LIVE The 47 storey Salomon Brothers building close to the World Trade Centre has also collapsed.

Image from video of WTC #7 standing as reporter says it has collapsed.

The Architects & Engineers for 9/11 Truth have formally filed a complaint regarding the National Institute of Standards and Technology (NIST) to retract and correct a 2008 report that concluded one of three World Trade Center buildings (WTC #7) collapsed because fire weakened the steel supporting it during the 9/11 attacks.

Robert Korol, McMaster University professor emeritus of civil engineering said, "The report notes that the outside frame was more flexible than the inside framing which is where the elevator shafts were." He continued, "Under the conditions described, the displacement of the outside steel would have been only one inch, not the 6.25" the NIST claimed and not enough to cause a near-simultaneous failure of every column in the building." Korol dismissed the NIST finding that heat from the fire caused the beams to 'walk off' their moorings stating, "It just didn't happen the way we have been told."

There is a rumor that the twin towers and WTC #7 are the only steel structure buildings to collapse due to fire. This is not entirely true. They were the only steel buildings to fall that also had a sprinkler system in place. The other buildings were:

Alexis Nihon Plaza Montreal, Canada

- Steel frame with composite steel beam and deck floors; fire resistant without sprinklers
- 15 floors, Office
- Oct. 26, 1986, after 5-hour fire, which then continued for 13 hours.
- Partial 11th floor collapse

One New York Plaza New York, NY, USA:

- Steel framing with reinforced concrete core, fire resistant with no sprinklers.
- 50 floors, Office
- August 5, 1970
- Connection bolts sheared during fire, causing several steel filler beams on the 33-34th floors to fall and rest on the bottom flanges of their supporting girders.

In both of these other buildings, they DID NOT COLLAPSE. They partially collapsed onto the floors below them. One must also consider that an airplane crashed into each World Trade Center (1 & 2), which could weaken the overall strength of the building. However, these buildings were designed to withstand a Boeing 707 crash without collapsing. The argument is not that they collapsed, it's in the manner of how they collapsed. They didn't 'topple' over due to the force of the airplanes hitting them, they literally collapsed, floor by floor, on top of each other into their own footprints. The steel was compromised by the airplanes, but not by the accompanying fire.

Steel melts at 2500 degrees Fahrenheit. Jet fuel burns between 800-1500 degrees Fahrenheit.

If you've ever seen the planned demolition of a skyscraper being brought down amidst other tall buildings surrounding it, what you have seen is the building collapsing in on itself, so as to not damage any of the buildings around. Watch the Trade Towers collapsing. Look familiar?

WAKE UP AMERICA

YOUR GOVERNMENT'S LYING TO YOU!

Big Pharma in America

Try turning on your television without seeing a commercial by Big Pharmacy. According to a report by eMarketer, in 2022, pharmaceutical and healthcare companies are expected to spend $11,680,000,000 on TV advertising in the United States, which represents approximately 9.7% of all TV advertising spent nationally. Incredibly, between the hours of 7:00 a.m. and midnight, nearly 30% of all commercials aired are either Big Pharma or Healthcare. Amazingly, this number increases to over 75% when aired on national television news programs such as ABC, CBS, NBC, CNN, FOX, Dateline, and 20/20. And it seems as if the side effects are 99.9% times worse than the disease or problem they are claiming to cure! To avoid any lawsuits, the names of those drugs will not be listed here, but one in particular mentions ALS as a possible side effect! Yes, you read that correctly, Lou Gehrig's Disease, a disease that robs the mind of the individual and tortures their life and the lives of their families. How and why would the FDA approve any drug that could cause such a debilitating condition? In 2020, the top 10 pharma Corporations combined to spend a total of $4,580,000,000 in TV advertising, slightly up from the $3,790,000,000 in 2019. With absolute certainty the revenues they realized from those campaigns far exceeded the spend.

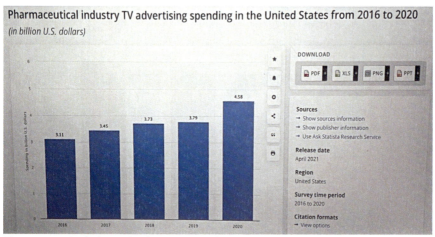

Pharmaceutical chart displaying spending 2016-2020.

The following ad was recently broadcast on FOX News. The medication being promoted reduces scrotal wrinkles. Is this horrendous affliction really a nationwide malaise? As always, the commercials are filled with people going to an amusement park, having a family reunion, going to a BBQ, or as this particular ad showed, a woman happily running through a field of flowers. How happy she must be that her significant other doesn't have nearly as many scrotal wrinkles. How exactly is this drug taken or used?

Evidently, she is very happy her significant other's genitalia isn't wrinkled.

For the price of a medication to reduce your scrotal wrinkles, the possible side effects advertised are incredible, let's take a look:

Side effects are rare* but may include: thoughts of suicide; actual suicide; severe bleeding from the rectum, eyes, nose, mouth, ears, or belly-button; catastrophic failure of the heart, brain, liver, kidneys, skin, or other organs necessary to life; spontaneous combustion or decomposition; stigmata; hyper or hyposexuality; unusual hair growth on the tongue, eyes, and/or fingertips; paranoia and delusions; sudden Anatidaephobia; lupus; death-by-a-thousand-cuts; and mild constipation.

If you experience any of these side effects, talk to your doctor. <mark>*about increasing your dose!*</mark>

*Note: The word 'rare' has been purchased and redefined by Glaxon-Smith-Pfizer-Bayer-Fox News Corporation and is subject to daily revision. Daily revision? Rare is a conjoined twins' birth, rare is an animal born with an additional leg. Besides all the horrible side effects, our favorite is bleeding from the bellybutton. Besides birth, when has this ever happened? Spontaneous combustion or decomposition? Unusual hair growth on your tongue? Mild constipation would be the least of my worries. Did constipation ever kill anyone?

So, the logical question is, why all the television ads by Big Pharmacy? The answer is really quite simple. With Big Pharmacy, there is more money in treating the disease than finding the cure. Your authors believe there may already be a cure for most of the maladies that afflict the human race, but making those cures available to anyone who needed them would eventually put Big Pharma out of business. This paradox translates across a broad spectrum of services we take for granted every day. We have the technology where airplanes can completely take off, fly, and land, without a pilot being in the cockpit. Why do we not have this technology in automobiles? Simple, the insurance, original equipment manufacturers, auto parts and replacement manufacturers, and auto/body repair shops will not allow us to implement this technology. There would be no payments necessary for auto insurance if there never were any accidents. (there would also be no more drunk drivers, no more distracted drivers, no more elderly and inattentive divers, no irresponsible teen drivers and etc., but that would cost the wrong people and governments a lot of money, so it will never happen.) It's all a rich man's trick, and like P.T. Barnum said, "there's a sucker born every minute." We allow the wool to be pulled over our eyes without asking why. We are sheep. As long as we have a car in the driveway, a roof over our heads, food in the pantry, decent health and life insurance, and a little money in the bank, who are we to question our government? We had better soon. Otherwise, we may find that the successes and liberties we take for granted will be taken away from us. It can and will happen. As noted radio host Neal Boortz said often, "Once the Government takes something away, you'll never get it back again."

Although the U.S. government is severely flawed, it is still the best form of government in the world. Only upon dissection should the government be adjusted. Thomas Jefferson once said, "Politics is not a Profession." Political reform is vastly needed if the United States is to ever to return to her former glory. How can an elected congressperson begin a two-year term with a salary of $174,000 a

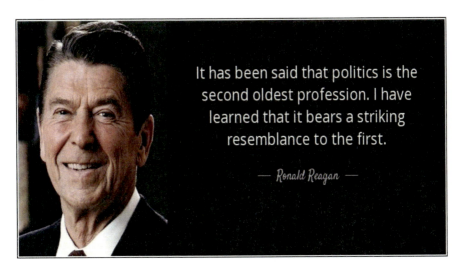

It has been said that politics is the second oldest profession. I have learned that it bears a striking resemblance to the first.

— *Ronald Reagan* —

year and leave office after two years a multi-millionaire? Term limits need to be implemented. The 22nd Amendment to the Constitution states that no President can hold office longer than two terms or ten years if he assumes the role of President with less than two years remaining on his predecessor's term. The same needs to be done to all levels of political office. These are our suggestions:

Governors are voted every four years
to a maximum of two terms.

Congressional seats are voted every two years
to a maximum of two terms.

Senatorial seats are voted every six years
to a maximum of two terms.

Vice President and President are voted every four years,
again, to a maximum of two terms.

Supreme Court justices a maximum of eight years,
Chief Justice a maximum of twelve years.

If you have served your maximum four years in Congress, then you need to run for state Governor. Once you have expired in these roles you can run for Senate. Obviously, you can run for any office at any time, but term limits need to be instituted if we are to ever to eliminate career politicians. Should the recent allegations against supreme court justice Clarence Thomas and his wife accepting money for education of their nephew, consulting fees, and etc., be ignored? Justice Kavanaugh and others have also lied about their backgrounds just to be given a 'get out of jail free' card after their nomination is confirmed. Just like Loyd Jowers, you can lie and deny all you want, but when the truth proves otherwise, you must face the facts. Just because a Supreme Court justice gets confirmed doesn't mean they have a free ride the rest of their lives. What makes them above the law? Especially on the Supreme Court! Also, as a country, we need to revisit our Presidential elections. Before 1804, whichever party was elected President, the other party was Vice-President. This needs to be considered. The United States can be the world leader in democracy. First, we have to be honest with ourselves. Second, we need to be honest to the people we represent. And finally, we need Presidential oversight to examine the previous administration to make sure they are honest and forthright. If errors or misjudgments are discovered, the previous President should lose their pension and be barred from speaking engagements. Together the American people can do better. Together we must.

A government that would condone and participate in the assassinations of world leaders and help orchestrate the deaths of visionary men like RFK, JFK and MLK – and hide the truth as to what really happened – is a government that must be stopped if we are ever to return to the country our forefathers envisioned.

Footnotes

The Death of A President

(a) Brothers—The Hidden History of the Kennedy Years, 2007, David Talbot.
(b) Mob Lawyer, 1994, Frank Ragano & Selwyn Raab.
(c) Personal interview with Paul O'Connor, Tampa, 1989.
(d) Personal interview with Tom Robinson, Arlington, VA, 1987.
(e) Jfklibrary.org. Charles Spalding interview 3/22/1969.
(f) Ibtimes.com, Joseph Lazarro, 12/20/13.
(g) One Hell of a Gamble: Khruschev, Castro and Kennedy 1958-1964, Aleksandr Fusenko, Timothy Naftali, 1998.
(h) American Experience, PBS, 2008.

Senator From New York

(a) 1964 United States Senate election in New York, Wikipedia.
(b) Americanbar.org
(c) Moazedi.blogspot.com, Diversity is Beautiful, April 4, 2017

The Road to California

(a) CBS Sunday Morning, Pete Hamill Letter to RFK, 2018.
(b) Jfklibrary.org, Robert F. Kennedy speech, 3/16/1968.
(c) Jfklibrary.org, Robert F. Kennedy speech, 4/4/1968.

The Ambassador Hotel

(a) Jns.org, Volume 130, issue 5, June 2018.
(b) Bobby and Jackie—A Love Story, C. David Heymann, 2009

Rats In The Woodpile

(a) Radaronline.com
(b) News.bbc.co.uk
(c) Who killed Bobby; The Unsolved Murder of Robert Kennedy, Shane O'Sullivan, SkyHorse Publishing 2018
(d) Brothers: The Hidden History of The Kennedy Years, David Talbot, Free Press, 2008

Hail Cesar

(a) The Assassination of Robert F. Kennedy—A Searching Look at the Conspiracy and Cover-Up 1968-1978—Turner, Christian, Basic Books Publishing, 2006.
(b) The Robert F. Kennedy Assassination—New Revelations on the Conspiracy and Cover-Up 1968-1991, Philip Melanson, Shapolsky Publishing, 1991.
(c) A Lie Too Big to Fail, Lisa Pease, Feral House, 2018.
(d) The Assassination of Robert F. Kennedy—A Searching Look at the Conspiracy and Cover-Up 1968-1978—Turner, Christian, Basic Books Publishing, 2006.

LAPD & Media Complicity

(a) New York Times article, November 13, 2022.
(b) Los Angeles Times, Jan. 13, 2023.
(c) RFK Must Die, Shane O' Sullivan, 2007
(d) Los Angeles Free Press, Jeffrey Kaye, August 29-
September 4, 1975.
(e) UPI archives, Key RFK photo, report withheld by police,
Russell Snyder, April 22, 1988.
(f) Historynewsnetwork.org, Mel Ayton column
(g) The Washington Post, John Leyden, Jan. 26, 1992.

How Many Cooks Are in the Kitchen

(a) Lib.umassd.edu

Medical Reports of Robert F. Kennedy

(a) Thesmokinggun.com

RFK Eulogy by Edward Kennedy

(a) Jfklibrary.org

Funeral Train

(a) RFK Funeral Train, Paul Fusco, 2001, Dewi Lewis
Publishing.

What May Have Been

(a) Jfklibrary.org